To FRROFY

(SAPIENTIA ET VIRTUS)

MACDONALD

SLAINTÉ

Stevie

TANGO 1-1

Dedication

I dedicate this book to my family and friends who inspired me to write it. To my children and grandchildren. To my brother LRPs who were killed in action while serving with our unit. A special thanks to my wife Maria Angeles Galan de Thayer, who has been an inspiration in my life and who has helped me in so many ways.

TANGO 1-1

9TH INFANTRY DIVISION
LRPS IN THE VIETNAM DELTA

JIM THAYER

Pen & Sword
MILITARY

AN IMPRINT OF PEN & SWORD BOOKS LTD.
YORKSHIRE – PHILADELPHIA

First published in Great Britain in 2020 by
PEN AND SWORD MILITARY
An imprint of
Pen & Sword Books Limited
Yorkshire – Philadelphia

ISBN 978 1 52675 858 3

A CIP catalogue record for this book is available from the British Library.

Typeset in Times New Roman 11.5/14 by
Aura Technology and Software Services, India.
Printed and bound in the UK by TJ International, Padstow, Cornwall.

Pen & Sword Books Limited incorporates the imprints of Atlas, Archaeology,
Aviation, Discovery, Family History, Fiction, History, Maritime, Military, Military
Classics, Politics, Select, Transport, True Crime, Air World, Frontline Publishing,
Leo Cooper, Remember When, Seaforth Publishing, The Praetorian Press,
Wharncliffe Local History, Wharncliffe Transport, Wharncliffe True Crime and
White Owl.

For a complete list of Pen & Sword titles please contact
PEN & SWORD BOOKS LIMITED
47 Church Street, Barnsley, South Yorkshire S70 2AS, United Kingdom
E-mail: enquiries@pen-and-sword.co.uk
Website: www.pen-and-sword.co.uk

Or
PEN AND SWORD BOOKS
1950 Lawrence Rd, Havertown, PA 19083, USA
E-mail: Uspen-and-sword@casematepublishers.com
Website: www.penandswordbooks.com

Contents

Prologue

Long Range Patrol

The men I am writing about could well have been the boy next door or the gentle blond-haired kid from the corner supermarket of not so long ago. The 'boys' are bound together by their trade. They are all volunteers. They are in the spine-tingling, brain-twisting, nerve-wracking business of Long Range Patrolling. They vary in age from 18 to 30. These men operate in precision movements, like walking through a jungle quietly and being able to tell whether a man or an animal is moving through the brush without seeing the cause of movement. They can sit in an ambush for hours without moving a muscle except to ease the safety off the automatic weapon in their hand at the first sign of trouble. These men are good because they have to be to survive. Called LRPs for short, they are despised, respected, admired and sometimes thought to be a little short on brains by those who watch from the sidelines as a team starts out on another mission to seek out the enemy. They are men who can take a baby or small child in their arms and make them stop crying. They share their last smoke, last ration of food, last canteen of water, kind in some ways, deadly in others. They are men who believe in their country, freedom, and fellow men. They are a new kind of soldier in a new type of warfare. They may look the same as any one you may have seen in a peace march, draft card burning or any other demonstration, but they are different. Just look in their eyes. Better yet, just ask them, for they are men. These men stand out in a crowd of soldiers; it is not just their tiger fatigues but the way they walk, talk and stand. You know they are proud because they are members of the Long Range Patrol.

Article from *Stars and Stripes*
Early 1968, author unknown

Foreword

My name is Robert Hill, and I served in the 9th Infantry Division's Long Range Patrol Company from November 1968 until late February 1969. I first served as Platoon Leader, then Commanding Officer of D Company, 6th Battalion, 31st Infantry. On 20 November 1968, after an interview with Captain Dale Dickey, E Company, 50th Infantry (LRP) Commanding Officer, I transferred into the unit. E Company was the organic long range patrol unit for the 9th Infantry Division.

The LRPs used different tactics, different weapons and had a completely different attitude than what I had experienced with the Infantry. LRPs worked in small teams of four to six men, far from any other friendly units, often out toward the edges of the Division's Area of Operations. All LRPs were volunteers, highly-trained, self-motivated, and if not totally without fear, nearly so. LRPs did not remain in a landing zone when they were inserted on a patrol. As the lift ship departed the LZ, the team would sprint for the cover of the nearest tree-line. They didn't smoke at night, they didn't sleep very much in the field, and when they spoke to each other or talked on the radio, it was always in a hushed whisper. Hand signals replaced verbal commands. Their actions were those of warriors who wanted to find the enemy, and when they felt they had the tactical advantage, would kill or capture them. Needless to say, I was very impressed with the way they operated.

I first met Sergeant Jim Thayer when he returned to the unit from R&R in Hawaii. I was the OIC (Officer in Charge) of the LRP unit stationed at the 3rd Brigade base camp at Tan An. We got to know each other well over the next few weeks. Jim had a Vietnamese soldier, a PRU (Provisional Reconnaissance Unit) who went everywhere that Jim went, which meant that Jim always had an interpreter with him, someone who knew the terrain, the people and who was acutely knowledgeable of the enemy's tactics. This proved to be a huge advantage to Jim and his team, since so few Americans ever understood the enemy's methods and operational tactics.

FOREWORD

A major who I knew from the 6th of the 31st Infantry asked me one day if I had anyone in my command who could interrogate a VC prisoner. The Brigade Intel people had no luck getting any information out of him. I told him that I would find somebody and went straight to see Jim Thayer. I asked him if he and his PRU would agree to have a talk with this POW. To this day I have no idea what they did or said to him, as he was unmarked at the end of the interrogation, but suddenly he became a wealth of information, giving up the location of a regimental-sized NVA unit well outside Tan An. Jim Thayer swore to me that they never touched the guy.

Brigade wanted us to check out the Intel and insert one of our teams to verify the location of the enemy. I asked Jim Thayer to go in with his team and he agreed. The enemy was there alright, and immediately Jim's team came under heavy rifle, machine-gun and RPG fire. Jim's RTO, Specialist Fourth Class Richard Bellwood, was killed. Jim's wristwatch and wrist compass were shot off his arm and his canteen took a round causing water to run down his hip and leg, which at the time he figured was blood from a bullet wound. I was at the Brigade Tactical Operations Center monitoring the radio and as soon as Jim called in a contact, I called for helicopter gunship support. The gunships gave a medevac helicopter the opportunity to get in and extract Jim, who had sustained a severe shoulder wound, the dying Bellwood, and the remainder of the team. Richard Bellwood's name is on the Vietnam Memorial Wall in Washington, DC with those of many other brave men.

Sergeant Thayer was transferred to the 3rd Field Hospital in Saigon where doctors performed surgery on his shoulder wound. The next day he was scheduled for transfer to a hospital in Japan. But first, Major General Julian Ewell, Commanding Officer of the 9th Infantry Division, along with Captain Dickey and myself watched as Jim was awarded the Silver Star, Purple Heart and a promotion to Staff Sergeant E-6.

I hope my introduction serves to give you at least a partial understanding of how LRPs operated during the war in Vietnam, the risks they took and the obstacles they overcame.

I am very proud of being accepted by these courageous soldiers and to have served as their leader. They were and still are some of the bravest men I have ever known, especially Jim Thayer, who stood out among other brave men as a man, a leader, and a combat soldier.

Robert M. Hill
Captain, Infantry
USAR (Retired)

ix

Introduction

The following is the story of my service with E Company, 50th Inf. (LRP) and E Company 75th Inf. (Ranger) in South Vietnam during the years 1968–69.

We were unique and somewhat different to the other Long-Range Patrol/Ranger units that served during the Vietnam War. There were several reasons for this. I'll endeavor to explain it here so that you will understand the reason why when you read my story.

Our area of operations was in the Mekong Delta of South Vietnam. The Delta was heavily populated and served as the 'breadbasket' for the entire nation. It consisted of thousands of square miles of rice paddies and hundreds of small farming hamlets and villages. The terrain was mostly level with standing water everywhere. The vegetation consisted primarily of reeds, thick grass, bamboo, narrow tree-lines and small expanses of dense, impenetrable jungle. Roads were rare, with canals and rivers the primary sources of travel.

The enemy we fought were usually local guerrilla units, 'Viet Cong' whose soldiers knew the area much better than we did. It was a distinct advantage for them. They mingled with the civilian population during the day, wore no uniforms and operated against us mainly during the hours of darkness. They deployed enormous numbers of booby-traps to impede our operations and cause heavy casualties among our forces. Their tactics were typically hit and run, and they seldom stood and fought.

We also encountered main force VC units. These were full-time soldiers who operated in larger, more organized elements and fought more conventional battles than the local VC. Occasionally, we ran into North Vietnamese Army units, more frequently as we eliminated the local VC and the war progressed. These were well-equipped, well-trained military forces that would usually stand and fight when encountered.

INTRODUCTION

The watery terrain made standard long-range reconnaissance operations impractical. Movement during daylight hours was difficult due to the lack of cover and concealment, and the large numbers of civilians moving about in the countryside. The length of our patrols was severely limited due to constant exposure to the wet terrain. The boots that our troops wore in the field kept their feet wet for extended periods of time, which quickly brought on immersion foot, trench foot and a variety of infections.

Most of our missions lasted from a few hours to less than two days, again dictated by the lack of cover, exposure to moisture, or being compromised by civilians who would often report our presence to the local VC forces.

The 9th Infantry Division lacked the aviation assets of many other American divisions serving throughout the country. This fact not only had a definite bearing on our overflights, insertions and extractions, but it also limited our ability to call for gunship support when in contact with the enemy. Infantry units engaged in larger, more sustained battles had priority over the air assets that were available.

Parakeet flights involved one of our teams aboard a Huey helicopter circling at altitude while an LOH (Light Observation Helicopter) scout flew at low level to flush enemy troops into the open. Once this was achieved, the Huey would drop off the team to engage and destroy them. The open terrain in the Delta facilitated this type of operation. Far from being a 'typical' long range patrol operation, it proved to be very effective in our area of operations. There were times when our teams would run two or more Parakeet flights in a single day. In the long run, it was not unusual for a 9th Division LRP/Ranger to participate in 100 or more missions during a single one-year tour in Vietnam, something that was unheard of in the other Long Range Patrol and Ranger companies that saw service in-country.

The events, characters and descriptions in my book come from memories both good and bad. While serving in Vietnam I liked what I did and always felt self-confident in my actions and the decisions I made, and I firmly believe that my self-confidence was passed on to the men I worked with and led in the field.

Men who serve together in combat form a very special bond, unlike that of any other profession. When you eat together, sleep together and cover each other in combat you become very close. It is the reason that one soldier often gives his life for another. This is the reason why we still call each other 'Brother' years after our service ended. That devout sense of brotherhood never dies. To this very day I still feel especially close to the men I served with in Vietnam. It is always a 'special' experience to see them again at reunions, rallies or just talk with them on the phone.

There were times in combat when I may have been scared, but never once did I let it interfere with the performance of my duties. I was true to myself, my unit and my brothers-in-arms. During my years in the military I always attempted to do every job to the best of my ability. Doing anything less would have been detrimental to my character and my sense of honor. My story begins with my re-enlistment in the US Army and ends with my discharge at Fort Leonard Wood, Missouri. I endeavored to recreate the more memorable events from my time served in Vietnam. The stories and events are as accurate as the memory of an old warrior can recall. Whenever possible, I corroborated the facts with surviving members of my unit. Combat is never something warriors enjoy talking about, but these stories need to be told, lest they be forgotten forever. We owe that to posterity. I truly hope that my story enables the reader to understand the types of operations we ran, the hardships we endured and the sacrifices we made, both the good times and the bad. Although *Tango 1-1* is 'my' story, it is also the story of the courageous young men who lived it with me. May their legacy endure forever.

Chapter One

Like thousands of foreign soldiers before me, my first impression of Vietnam was the blast-furnace heat and the nauseating odor of human feces that hijacked my senses as I stepped from the Boeing 707 onto the top step of the stair ramp.

It was July 1968 and I was into my second enlistment in the US Army. I had previously served three years, attaining the rank of sergeant, but had decided to get out at the end of my enlistment due to extreme pressure from both my parents and my wife. I had lost an older brother in the Second World War and another of my brothers was on active duty serving as an Army colonel. With the war in Vietnam showing no signs of ending soon, my family didn't want to see another Thayer go into battle. I had discovered that I missed the military life almost immediately upon being discharged. The routine, the camaraderie, the lifestyle were impossible to replace on the outside. Despite threats and pleas from my family and friends, I finally made the decision to give the military another go and re-enlisted.

I lost a stripe due to the lapse in service and had to rejoin as a Specialist Fourth Class. When I signed the re-enlistment forms, I also volunteered for an assignment to Vietnam. I'd had enough of Stateside duty and wanted to test myself in the arena of combat. My goal was to get into one of the long-range reconnaissance units that I had heard so many stories about during my previous enlistment. LRPs were highly-trained, heavily-armed teams of five to six men that operated deep behind enemy lines. They relied heavily on stealth and the element of surprise to accomplish their missions. The word was out that you had to be insane to go into enemy territory with so few men, but stories of their daring operations were often discussed among soldiers returning from Vietnam, and the high degree of respect and blatant admiration for these silent warriors was readily apparent. I had picked up on some of these tales when I was stationed at the Presidio in San Francisco. They sounded so exciting that I immediately found myself yearning to be a part of such a unit. I also realized that it would be much easier getting promotions in a specialized unit. Promotions and serving in a combat zone meant more money and not having to pay income taxes. I was a married man with a baby daughter to provide for, so the additional funds would help support my family.

Shortly after deplaning on our arrival in South Vietnam, we were herded from Tan Son Nhut Air Base in Saigon to a line of waiting olive drab military buses. As we stowed our luggage and filed aboard, we couldn't help but notice the heavy wire screens welded over the windows. One of the returning veterans with us saw the puzzled looks on our faces and told us that they were put there to prevent VC guerrillas from tossing frags in the windows as we drove through the congested areas on our way to the Replacement Center. The enemy was adept at taking advantage of any situation where they could inflict mass casualties, then escape in the resulting confusion. It had happened on many occasions, especially around Saigon. That little bit of insight convinced all of us 'cherries' that we had finally arrived in the war zone.

We convoyed to the 90th Replacement Center at Long Binh a few miles outside Saigon. Our heads were on swivels as we took in the sights of this strange new country. The buildings along the roads appeared to be a patchwork of French colonial architecture, Indo-Chinese structures, small working-class homes that appeared to be made of some type of stucco, and finally large numbers of shanties made from cast-off materials, flattened tin cans and anything else that might serve to keep out the weather.

When we reached the 90th Replacement Center, we disembarked from the buses, secured our gear and immediately assembled into a formation, where a waiting cadre greeted us and collected our paperwork. They welcomed us to Vietnam, gave us some basic instructions and assigned us to temporary barracks nearby. A short time later, we were summoned back outside to another formation and assigned work details. The Army had long ago learned that keeping soldiers busy prevented them from finding things to do that might get them into trouble. The mandatory formations and work details would become the general routine while we waited for our orders to come down assigning us to a permanent unit somewhere in South Vietnam.

CHAPTER ONE

My first full day in-country found me on KP duty, helping the line cooks prepare and serve the three meals of the day. It proved to be a long thirteen-hour shift with few breaks to relax or catch one's breath. When it finally came to an end and I was on my way back to my barracks all greasy and sweaty, I promised myself that it wouldn't happen again if I could help it. I made sure over the next few days while attending orientation classes that I would find whatever excuses I could come up with for not making the mandatory morning formations where the work details were assigned.

I knew I wouldn't be at the Replacement Center long enough to make any friends. However, I did manage to strike up conversations with a few guys. I remember one of them, a guy from the East Coast who was overly anxious about being assigned to an infantry unit. He told me that he knew he wasn't going to make it back home alive. There was no amount of reasoning with him. I tried to ease his mind by telling him he had just as good a chance of surviving as anyone else, to just do what he had been trained to do, listen to the veterans, and not worry about anything else. I don't know if my advice helped him or not, but I knew that harboring those kinds of negative thoughts about dying in battle would be a handicap to him if he continued to let them control his mind.

The orientation classes were designed to make us aware of the dangers that existed in what would become our home for the next twelve months. We were warned about buying Cokes, homemade bread or other foodstuffs from the civilian vendors who seemed to be everywhere. The enemy had been known to place foreign objects like finely ground glass, bits of metal or even battery acid in sodas and foodstuffs, which would likely result in a trip to the hospital or to Graves Registration for those foolish enough to consume them. The instructors demonstrated several types of Viet Cong booby-traps the enemy employed that were designed to maim or kill unwary soldiers: things like punji pits, Malayan whips, grenades hooked to trip-wires, pressure mines, bamboo vipers hidden in coconuts and gourds, anti-personnel mines, etc. The VC had spent years fighting the Japanese and the French. They had developed their own form of guerrilla warfare and were quite adept at causing casualties among their enemies without risk to themselves. It was an eye-opening revelation for all of us 'cherries' who had been trained to confront the enemy face-to-face in battle. Guerrilla warfare of this type was not

3

what we had prepared for in BCT (Basic Combat Training) and AIT (Advanced Individual Training). We would have to learn quickly.

We were also warned to avoid any place that was marked 'off-limits' to American servicemen, and to stay out of the towns and villages, especially at night. The instructors told us that the VC lived among the civilian population during the day, then formed up at night to attack allied bases and set up their booby-traps. The darkness belonged to 'Charlie' and we were to respect that if we wanted to survive our year in-country. There were so many ways to die in this lush, humid land that one should never put himself in danger by taking unnecessary or foolish risks.

The instructors cautioned us to avoid the 'red light' districts found in most of the larger towns and cities. They informed us that there were more types of venereal diseases found in Indo-China than any other place in the world, especially the dreaded, highly-contagious 'Black Syphilis', a disease so terrible that if you came down with it, you'd have to be quarantined on an island in the South China Sea for the rest of your life. It was highly contagious and there was no cure for it once you got it. None of us realized at the time that most of these stories had been contrived by the cadre to keep us out of areas that had been posted as 'off-limits' to military personnel. Although these threats worked for a while, it didn't take long for us lusty young Americans to overcome our fears, first out of curiosity, then through the outright boldness of youth.

On my fifth day at the 90th Replacement Center, my orders came down assigning me to the 9th Infantry Division at Bear Cat. I knew about the 9th Infantry Division from stories I had read about it during the Second World War. The unit was highly-respected and I was pleased to find myself assigned to it. I rushed to gather my gear and turn in my bedding so that I could catch a truck for the thirty-minute ride out to the Division's base camp.

I arrived at Bear Cat and was immediately assigned to the 9th Division's Replacement Company along with several other new arrivals. Bear Cat was a large base camp located on a slightly higher piece of ground than the surrounding terrain. A dense jungle lay beyond the perimeter of the base camp with much of the vegetation cleared back from the perimeter wire for several hundred meters. Not long after I reported in, I discovered that I wouldn't be in Bear Cat for long. The Division was in the process of relocating to Dong Tam, south of Saigon in the northern part of the Mekong Delta, to be closer to its main Area of Operations.

CHAPTER ONE

I didn't waste any time before volunteering for the Division's long range patrol unit. Known as E Company, 50th Infantry (LRP), the unit was already scattered between Bear Cat and Dong Tam. It was an all-volunteer outfit, and a request to join it superseded orders to report to any other unit in the Division. When I told the personnel specialist at the Replacement Company that I wanted to volunteer for the LRPs, he gave me a look that sent a chill running up my back. Although he didn't say anything against my decision, it was obvious that he thought I was either mentally impaired or had some sort of insatiable death wish. My orders came down a couple of days later assigning me to the Division's Long Range Patrol unit.

I grabbed my gear and reported to E Company's orderly room a few hundred meters from the Replacement Company. When I checked in and handed my paperwork to the company clerk, I was informed that part of the unit had already moved to Dong Tam, and it wouldn't be long before the rest of the company left Bear Cat to join them there. He cautioned me against getting too comfortable because I wouldn't be in Bear Cat long enough to get a new set of clean sheets.

I was told to report to my platoon sergeant to find out where I could drop my gear. When I located him a short time later, he seemed like a decent sort, a man you could talk to, so I took the opportunity to ask him what to expect as an LRP. He put his hand on my shoulder, smiled and said: 'Your TL [team leader] will tell you everything you need to know after you get assigned to a team.'

I was only at Bear Cat for a couple of weeks. I filled my time pulling police calls through the company area, shooting the bull with other recently-arrived replacements, and just generally goofing off while we waited for our opportunity to rejoin the rest of the company.

The word finally came down that Robert Loehlein, Pat Lafferty and I were to pack our bags and get out to the airstrip to catch a flight down to Dong Tam. The three of us hurriedly grabbed our gear, caught a ride out to the PSP airstrip inside the base camp and climbed aboard a waiting C-7 Caribou for the short hop to the Division's new base camp at Dong Tam.

Dong Tam proved to be nothing like Bear Cat. The newly-constructed base sprawled over a large area of dry ground along the east side of the Mekong River 7 kilometers west of the town of My Tho. The encampment was surrounded by a vast expanse of marshy terrain that extended as far as the eye could see. The Navy had begun work on the site in 1966, reclaiming 600 acres of swamp land by dredging the river bottom to build up the site for the Division's new base camp. Thanks to the Seabees, Dong Tam was relatively high and dry. General William Westmoreland had selected the site himself. He wanted it located right in the heart of the Mekong Delta where the 9th Division would be operating to wrest control of the northern delta from the Viet Cong forces who freely operated throughout the area. In January 1967, VC sappers sank the dredge ship *Jamaica Bay* in a futile attempt to halt construction on the site. MACV rushed the 3rd Battalion, 60th Infantry from Bear Cat to provide security for the base as construction continued, and three months later, the 9th Infantry Division's 2nd Brigade relocated from Bear Cat to Dong Tam to begin operations in the area surrounding the new base camp.

A month later, the US Navy's River Assault Squadron 9 arrived at Dong Tam to support the 2nd Brigade's activities, and in June the Navy's River Assault Squadron 11 joined its sister unit and along with the 9th Division's 2nd Brigade, formed the Mobile Riverine Force (MRF) to conduct joint operations throughout the Delta. The base eventually grew to 12 square miles with a 500ft airstrip and a slack-water harbor at the end of a canal that ran from the river back into the safety of the base camp.

Our Caribou screeched to a halt on the short PSP runway inside the Dong Tam perimeter. Loehlein, Lafferty and I shouldered our gear and strode down the aircraft's rear ramp onto the hot, steel-planked runway. We asked a couple of 9th Division soldiers on a nearby work detail where the Long Range Patrol compound was located and were directed to an area on the opposite side of the base camp away from the river. One of the soldiers told us: 'It's right next to the Division's generator station. You can't miss it.' We thanked him and walked to the edge of the airstrip and hitched a ride on a passing three-quarter-ton truck.

Five minutes later the truck pulled to the side of the road to let us out in front of the E Company, 50th Infantry compound. We shouldered our duffle bags and walked up to the first building. It was labeled 'Supply' and was a rather large single-story wooden building with the supply area in the center of the structure. On one end of the building were rooms where I imagined the supply sergeant and his clerks lived. On the other end was the LRP Club/Canteen which served as a place to get a cold beer or soda, and a few snacks like canned beans and weenies,

CHAPTER ONE

Vienna sausages, cheese crackers, etc. The club also had a pool table for the pleasure of the troops. Next to the club was the unit's headquarters or orderly room where the commanding officer, the company clerks and the operations staff worked. The company commander had a private room in the rear where he slept. Beyond the orderly room was a large open area with bleachers set up at the rear. It appeared to be a training and briefing area. Next to the bleachers was a homemade movie screen that was probably used to show films at night that were requisitioned from Special Services. Beyond the training area was yet another open area. It was next to a large two-story wooden barracks with a large sandbagged bunker on the near side of the building. A passing LRP saw us looking at the open ground and pointed out that this was the site for a second barracks building to be constructed in the immediate future.

After familiarizing ourselves with the layout of the LRP compound, we reported in to the company clerk in the orderly room. We handed him our paperwork and waited patiently as he checked us off his roster. When he was satisfied that everything was in order, he told us to go back to the barracks and grab some empty bunks on the second floor. We asked him why the second floor, and he told us that the first floor was reserved for officers and NCOs, E-6 and above. The upper floor was an open bay and was where the 'ranks' slept. He added: 'Before you go to the barracks, stop by Supply and turn in your helmet and flak jacket… you won't be needing those here in the LRPs.'

We left the orderly room for the short walk to Supply. I couldn't help but notice the same thick, nauseating smell in the air that had greeted me when I had landed at Tan Son Nhut Air Base three weeks earlier. I discovered later that day that the odor came from the US Army's weekly routine of incinerating the human waste in the metal burn barrels stowed beneath the seats in the wooden outhouses found on nearly every military installation in-country. Someone had determined that it was the only 'sanitary' method for disposing of the fecal deposits made by nearly a half-million Americans in uniform serving in South Vietnam. I don't know how sanitary it was for the poor soldiers who had to pour diesel fuel in the half-drums, light it, then stir it occasionally with a metal fence post until it was reduced to ash. The odiferous by-product resulting from the waste cremation would take a long, long time to get used to.

As the company clerk had told us, the Supply Sergeant ordered us to turn in our steel 'pots' and flak jackets. He then ordered us to read off the serial numbers on our M16s. After verifying that these were the same weapons that we had been issued in Bear Cat, he cautioned us: 'Use any kind of weapon you chose out in the boonies, but whatever you do, make sure that weapon you just registered is the same weapon you turn in when you leave country. There will be hell to pay if you don't have it.'

When we had finished turning in our unneeded gear, I enquired if the Supply Sergeant might need anyone else to work in the Supply room. I told him that I had served in Supply at two of my previous duty stations during my prior enlistment, so I had plenty of experience. He thought for a moment, then nodded and said he would talk to the Commanding Officer about it and get back to me in the next day or two. I thanked him and the three of us stepped outside and headed for the barracks.

Halfway to the two-story building housing the LRPs, a young buck sergeant stopped us and said: 'Is one you guys named Thayer?' I said: 'Yes, that's me.' He smiled and offered his hand: 'My name is Roy Barley. My mother's maiden name was Thayer. We just might be related.' I nodded and said: 'Well how do you do, cuz? Good to meet ya.' Many years later, both of us would discover that we were indeed distant cousins.

I got to the barracks and found an empty bunk close to the door. I claimed it by tossing my duffle bag on top of the footlocker at the end of the bed. I reasoned that in case of a rocket attack, I wouldn't have as far to go to get to the bunker located out on the side of the building. I unrolled the mattress, made up the bunk with my poncho liner, and put my socks, underwear and extra fatigues in the footlocker. I located a few wooden ammo boxes and made up some shelves and a little desk to keep my personal items in.

The barracks building was a lot nicer than I had expected. It had been constructed on a concrete pad and seemed more than adequate for a military housing unit. There was electricity throughout the building, allowing some of the guys to have portable TVs, electric fans, hotplates and small refrigerators in their immediate areas. Many of the LRPs had erected short, half-wall partitions to afford them a little privacy and define their personal areas.

Weapons were hanging everywhere from nails driven into the walls of the barracks building. Most were M16s and CAR-15s, but there were several other interesting weapons as well. I spotted a couple of British Sterlings and British Sten guns hanging from their pegs. There was even a black M3 grease gun in the corner of one LRP's personal area.

The British guns fired 9mm rounds, while the American-made M3 fired .45 caliber rounds. There was quite a collection of Chi-Com and Soviet SKS carbines and AK-47s assault rifles which I assumed were war souvenirs. There were a couple of the M14 rifles I had trained with during my first enlistment and I even spotted a single M1 .30 caliber carbine lying on another LRP's footlocker.

One of the older LRPs saw me admiring the collection of weapons and shouted: 'Impressive, isn't it! This isn't all of them. There's a lot more up at the LRP compound at Tan An. Staff Sergeant Hyland Jones even has an old British Bren gun he takes out on patrols.' I gave him a big grin and said: 'You've got to be shittin' me! A Bren gun must weigh over 20lb. Nobody can hump a weapon that big without killin' himself.' The LRP laughed at my incredulity. 'You haven't met Jonesy yet. He's 6ft 6in and looks like an NFL lineman. That Bren's like a submachine gun in his hands.' He smiled and added:

> Once you get broken in, you can decide whatever weapon you want to take out on patrol. The choice will be yours. Some parties you go to might require different toys. That will be up to you. Just make sure you know how to use each one before you decide to take it out in the bush. A firefight is the wrong place to familiarize yourself with your weapon.

I thanked him for the info and the bit of wisdom. I had a lot to learn and made sure that I would commit every bit of information I received to memory.

I went over and took a seat on my bunk. I did a little last-minute soul-searching and decided that I had made a mistake with the Supply Sergeant. I don't know why I had blurted out my desire to work in Supply. My original decision to join the LRPs was for the adventure and the opportunity to make rank quicker. Neither would come to pass working as a lowly supply clerk. I quickly made up my mind to let the Supply Sergeant know of my change of heart the first chance I got.

A couple of days later, the company clerk stopped by the barracks and told me that the Company Commander, Captain Dale Dickey, wanted to see me in the orderly room. I tossed on a clean fatigue shirt and hurried to Headquarters as ordered. After reporting in, Captain Dickey told me to have a seat. He wasted little time before asking: 'Thayer, it says in your file that you have experience in construction.' I answered: 'Yes, sir. After I graduated from high school, I worked for a company that built houses. I worked there for a year before I enlisted in the Army the first time.' He nodded approvingly and continued: 'Good! We're getting ready to build a new barracks next to the existing one and I want you to head up the project as the construction foreman. No one else here has enough experience to supervise the construction.' I said: 'Yes, sir, anything I can do to help.' Sometimes I speak before thinking. This was one of those times.

Construction began the next day. We poured a large concrete pad and set the sill plates. Then we framed the outer walls and set them in place, enclosing the first floor. Things seem to go well at first, except I was having a personal issue giving instructions to fellow workers who outranked me. It wasn't anything they did or said, but it was still bothering the hell out of me. After a few days as job foreman, I went back to Captain Dickey and told him my problem and requested to be pulled off the construction job and assigned to a team. He seemed disappointed to be losing his construction foreman, but said that he understood how I felt and immediately assigned me to one of the unit's undermanned long range patrols.

Chapter Two

I went out on a couple of missions with two different teams over the next two weeks. Each of the missions was brief and proved uneventful. We encountered no enemy troops, nor did we discover any sign that they had been in the area. However, the excitement I felt during the helicopter insertions was something I had never before experienced. It was exhilarating to sit on the outside edge of the cabin floor with my feet dangling above the skids, anticipating the right moment to leap from the chopper into hostile country. Even though we didn't see anything or make contact with the enemy during either patrol, the fact that we were on the ground in 'Indian country' was enough to keep me excited and on the tips of my toes. Operating with men who were self-motivated, dedicated professionals made me realize that I had indeed made the right choice in coming to the LRPs. I would never regret my decision.

After I returned from my second mission, Sergeant 'Pancho' Alire came to see me to let me know that I was being permanently assigned to his team, Tango 1-1. I was overjoyed. I was no longer a 'floater', but actually the member of a team.

I reported to the section of barracks assigned to Team 1-1. Alire was there waiting for me with his assistant team leader, Sergeant Bob Pegram. Alire introduced us, then asked where I was from. When I told them I was from Arkansas, he proudly announced that he was from New Mexico and that his family had been in the United States long before the Revolutionary War. Pegram said that he had grown up on the West Coast in California and had spent his youth surfing in the Pacific Ocean. Both men appeared intelligent, personable and were natural leaders. Both had been in-country long enough to be experienced operators in the field. They seemed pleased to have me on their team, and quickly introduced me to the other members of Team 1-1, Specialist Fourth Class Dan Bien, Specialist Fourth Class Mike O'Day and Private First-Class Jesse

DeLeon. They appeared to be a great bunch of guys and I looked forward to joining them on their next mission.

I had already decided that not only did I like working in the field with a small team of warriors, but that I happened to be pretty darned good at it. Growing up as a youth out in the country – hunting, camping, fishing and hiking – had prepared me well for this dangerous new profession I had chosen. I knew that I had found my calling and I vowed to make the best of it.

I went out on several patrols during the first two weeks of September. Most were uneventful, which was fine with me because it gave me time to familiarize myself with the techniques that had already been mastered by my teammates. Most of the missions consisted of Alire, Pegram, Bien, O'Day, DeLeon and I, but occasionally other LRPs would fill in for one of the regulars. I was amazed how these outsiders seemed to fit seamlessly into the team during these patrols. It was almost as if they had all been trained by the same instructor. I hoped that there would be opportunities in the future for me to join other teams who were short of a man for a mission. It appeared to be the standard way the LRPs of the 9th Infantry Division operated.

In mid-September, Richard Bellwood arrived in the unit and was also assigned to Team 1-1. He was a New York City boy who had virtually no experience in the woods other than infrequent visits to Central Park, and he had never fired a weapon before joining the Army. Despite his inexperience, we hit it off immediately and soon became fast friends. It was especially nice for me because with Bellwood's arrival, I was no longer the 'new guy' on Tango 1-1. However, Richard proved to be a quick study, and before long he became a valued member of our team.

Not long after Bellwood arrived, Bob Loehlein, one of the guys I had come to the LRPs with, was killed on a mission. Like Bellwood, I had instantly hit it off with Loehlein. He was a friendly guy and we had shared the common experience of joining the LRPs at the same time. Now he was gone. I felt tremendous grief over his loss. He had been more to me than just another LRP. He had also been my friend. I began to understand why we had been advised not to make any close acquaintances while serving in-country. When your buddies were killed there was no time to grieve or mourn, or to even think about the relationship you had with them. Their death was something you had to put behind you immediately; store it away in that distant 'safe place' in your mind to be dealt with at another time, a time when you could afford to evaluate mortality without jeopardizing your own. Danger and death were our constant companions in Vietnam. They were everywhere: out in the field, in the base camp, in the air, on the water…everywhere. Dwelling on them made you more than just cognizant of their existence, it also made you too careful, too judgmental, too hesitant, which could very well prevent you from responding properly in a life-threatening situation. The knowledge that the next time it might be you that falls in battle could easily become a self-fulfilling prophesy.

The last two weeks in September were more of the same: brief forays into the bush to check out suspected enemy troop locations, routes of movement, possible mortar and rocket positions or reported supply caches. Team 1-1 found nothing of any significance and soon we began to question the sources of the Intel coming down from G-2 (Division Intelligence). The more experienced guys on the team told me that 'dead missions' breed complacency, affect your judgment and weaken your situational awareness. They all agreed that we needed that shot of adrenaline that only a 'contact' mission could provide. It made sense to me, but at that point in my tour I still had a lot of lessons to learn.

Chapter Three

On 10 September an Intel report arrived at G-2 claiming that a VC paymaster would be coming down the Van Co River in a sampan sometime during the next few days. One of my new friends, C.R. Mathis, told me that his team had been given the mission of intercepting this guy. G-2 wanted him captured alive if possible, believing he would be a wealth of information about the local VC regular forces in the area.

C.R.'s team immediately began training for the mission. Someone at G-4 (Division Logistics) managed to come up with a Boston whaler boat that was 24ft long by 10ft wide, close to the dimensions of a mid-sized sampan. The next day, the LRP team began practicing for an airborne intercept of the enemy boat. The plan was for a Huey, with the team aboard, to overtake the sampan as it was moving downstream. The aircraft would move to a hover just above it while two of the LRPs leaped from the skids into the slow-moving craft and subdued the occupants. The rest of the team would provide cover from inside the helicopter. It was a gutsy plan but the LRPs felt that it could be accomplished. After rehearsing the operation several times, the team satisfied themselves that it was definitely doable. Each member of the team donned shorts and T-shirts, threw a bandoleer of ammo over his shoulder, grabbed his weapon and climbed aboard a Huey for the short flight out to a fire base near the Van Co River. They would remain there until they received word that the sampan had been spotted.

They were posted at the fire support base for two days before an agent upriver sent word to G-2 that the target had been spotted and was on its way downstream. C.R.'s team quickly boarded their waiting Huey and flew upstream to intercept the sampan. Intel had reported that there were two suspected VC aboard the boat. The LRPs knew that they would very likely be armed. Speed and surprise had to be in their favor if they were to succeed in the mission without taking any casualties.

The river was nearly 200ft wide and there were hundreds of sampans trafficking up and down the waterway at any point in time during daylight hours. Picking the right sampan was critical to their success. They hoped that the agent's description of the enemy craft had been accurate.

Approaching the vicinity described by the agent, the aircraft commander indicated that a large, open sampan approaching from upstream was their target. He quickly dropped the aircraft toward the slow-moving boat and brought the chopper to a hover directly above the center of the watercraft. C.R. and one of his teammates were already positioned out on the skids as the aircraft moved in a few feet over the sampan. They wasted little time leaping to the deck directly on top of the two-man crew. Before the VC could recover, the two LRPs were on their feet pointing their weapons at the surprised enemy soldiers. Overhead, the helicopter lifted away from the boat and came to a safe hover 50ft above the sampan. While C.R.'s teammate kept the enemy soldiers covered, C.R. bound each man's hands and feet with 'high-speed' tape, then blindfolded and gagged them. Satisfied that both VC were secure, the two LRPs put their weapons aside and guided the sampan into the nearest shore. The helicopter landed in a clearing on the riverbank to drop off the rest of the team. The three men jumped from the chopper and moved quickly down to the sampan to assist their teammates. C.R. led the two POWs up the embankment to the waiting helicopter as his comrades began searching the boat for contraband. They quickly discovered a pair of AK-47s hidden under some bamboo matting, several loaded magazines and a large bundle of South Vietnamese piasters. BINGO! The team had hit the payload. The mission was now an unqualified success. They had captured the VC paymaster and his escort, liberated a couple of enemy weapons and acquired a rather large amount of money that would eventually be turned over to the South Vietnamese government, and they had accomplished it without firing a single shot.

A short time later, the helicopter reached Dong Tam and dropped C.R. and his two POWs off at the Brigade helipad. The young LRP was met there by a captain from G-2 and a pair of tough-looking MPs. The officer was dressed in starched fatigues and sported highly-polished boots. While the two MPs loaded the captured VC into the back of a waiting three-quarter-ton truck for the trip back to G-2, the Intel officer turned to C.R. and began to read him the riot act for his slovenly appearance and for being out of uniform. The LRP stood there stoically, letting the armchair commando vent. When the officer finally finished his tirade, C.R. saluted him without saying a word, then turned and climbed back aboard the waiting helicopter. The shocked officer started to stop him, but by then it was too late. C.R. was already airborne and on his way to the LRP helipad on the other side of the base camp. He had learned a long time ago how to deal with prima donnas.

All five members of the LRP team involved in the mission were later awarded Army Commendation medals with 'V' device for their roles in the successful capture of the VC paymaster. It had been a textbook operation.

Chapter Four

At the beginning of October, we received a warning order for a recon mission in an area about 5 miles outside the wire at Dong Tam. We were told that we would be inserted at 'last light' for an overnight patrol. The team leader informed us that we would be going in 'light' with only our web gear and weapons. Our web gear consisted of a canteen, ammo pouches, hand grenades, smoke grenades and a med kit. Our med kits held pressure bandages, field dressings, codeine (cough suppressant), aspirin (minor pain), Darvon (major pain), morphine syrettes (severe pain), tetracycline (antibiotic), polymagma (anti-diarrhetic), and dextroamphetamine (pep-pills used to keep one awake).

The patrol was made up of 'Poncho' Alire, Bob Pegram, Jesse DeLeon, Fred Myers, Richard Bellwood and me. Alire called me aside and told me that he wanted me to carry the team radio during the mission.

There would be no helicopters for this insertion. Instead we were to be inserted by means of an open-bed, open-cab three-quarter-ton truck, and would be extracted late the next day at a pre-designated point on the Mekong River by a Navy PBR (Patrol Boat River).

We met the vehicle an hour before dark at the pick-up point outside our barracks. The TL and ATL climbed into the open cab alongside the driver, a chunky Private First Class from one of the Transportation companies stationed at Dong Tam. Since I was carrying the radio, I decided it would be wise to stay as close to our team leader as I could, so I climbed up and sat on the back of the seat and squeezed my legs between Alire and Pegram. The rest of the team scrambled into the rear of the truck and took up seats facing out as we got under way.

The driver decided that this would be a great opportunity to see how fast the vehicle could go. It occurred to me that he was either overly concerned with dropping us off and getting back to the relative safety of Dong Tam before dusk, or that possibly he fancied himself a stock car driver. Whatever the reason, he kept the gas pedal touching the floorboard as we sped away from Dong Tam.

About 2 miles outside the wire, the driver took a hard left around a sharp curve, I swear to this day, on just two wheels. In a millisecond, several events occurred that would prove non-beneficial to my health and wellbeing. First, gravity decided that my perch on the back of the seat was far too high for my own good. Second, the additional weight of the PRC-25 radio strapped to my back agreed with gravity. Third, centrifugal force decided that it was unfair for gravity to have all the fun, and fourth, my sphincter, realizing that an untenable situation was rapidly developing, made a desperate but unsuccessful attempt to suck up a handful of the pebbled vinyl covering the seatback I had just been sitting on. During that brief millisecond, I became acutely aware that my demise was imminent.

My first point of contact with the hard surface of the road was the back of my head. Keep in mind that LRPs never wear helmets. Next point of contact was the radio which, although protecting my back from direct impact with the road bed, still managed to imprint itself rather deeply into the flesh covering my dorsal area. The fall momentarily knocked me unconscious, which prevented me from remembering the horror of my headfirst slide across the pavement and into the bottom of a rather deep irrigation ditch that ran alongside the road. When I awoke seconds later and discovered that I was still alive, I immediately began checking myself for broken bones and missing limbs. Fortunately, except for a few scrapes and bruises, an agonizing headache and a very sore back, I seemed to be relatively unscathed.

The truck driver, realizing that his load had suddenly gotten a bit lighter, succeeded in finally bringing the machine to a complete stop almost 100 meters down the road from where I had gone airborne. While I was still trying to get my bearings I heard, then saw, the three-quarter-ton truck backing up the hardtop and grinding to a halt just above the scene of my touch-down. I watched my teammates as they piled out of the vehicle and rushed to my side, asking if I was okay. I answered rather angrily: 'I just fell out of a damned truck doing 100 miles an hour and you want to know if I'm feeling okay?'

Despite the seriousness of the moment, they seemed relieved that I was still alive, and took the opportunity to have a hearty laugh at my expense. One of the guys even reached down and pulled the radio off my back, not to ease my pain, but to check and see if it had survived the fall. Amazingly, it still functioned. Even more amazingly, so did the guy who was wearing it. Alire and Pegram helped me to my feet and stood ready to catch me if I went down. Gingerly, I walked over to the truck and took three aspirins from my med kit for the pain and discomfort, then climbed slowly back up onto the truck where I threatened to kill the driver if he didn't slow down to a safer speed. Satisfied that he was taking my words seriously, I laid down on the floor in the back of the truck and remained there for the rest of the journey.

We continued to the drop-off point, where the driver came to a rather overly-controlled but gentle halt. He said not a word, nor did he look in my direction, but after we climbed down from the truck and moved into the heavy cover a few meters back from the road, he hurriedly turned the vehicle around and sped back toward Dong Tam, once again at a very high rate of speed.

We finished the overnight mission, seeing no sign of the enemy, and the next day we made our way to the shore of the nearby Mekong River where we called for an extraction. By that time, I was as sore as a person could get and still be able to move. My body was calling me a fool for not taking the truck back to Dong Tam the evening before to report to the medical facility.

A short time later, a Navy patrol boat pulled into the shore next to our hide site and brought us back to Dong Tam where everyone but Alire headed for our barracks. Alire patted me on the shoulder and told me to drop off my gear, then go and see the company medic to be checked out. He had been aware that although I had managed to finish the mission, I was feeling like the sole survivor of a very bad train wreck.

After looking me over, the medic informed me that I had sustained several pretty nasty contusions and a few massive bruises that were already turning a yellowish purple. He also stated that I had probably suffered a slight concussion to my brain pan when I head-butted the pavement. He ordered me to go to bed and stay there for the next four to five days, adding that time and rest were the only things that would heal my injuries and restore my health. He then gave me a handful of pain pills and told me to come and see him again if I ran out and still needed them. I asked him when he thought I might be able to rejoin the team. He looked at me like I had just confirmed his diagnosis of a concussion, then told me that I could go back to the field when I felt I was ready or in a week, whichever came last. I thanked him and walked stiffly back to the barracks. I hoped that the pills would relieve some of the aches and pains, and I figured that Mother Nature would have to take care of the rest.

When I got back to the barracks, my teammates were just coming in from cleaning their weapons and preparing their gear for the next mission. They asked me what the medic had said and when would I be ready to go out on patrol again. My pride got the best of me, and I told them the doc said I was fine, and they could count on me being ready the next time we got an op order. I was certain that I would be good to go in a day or two and if not, I would fake it. In the LRPs you didn't let your teammates down.

Chapter Five

On 6 October we received another op order from G-2, this time for a three-day recon mission along the Mekong River. The entire five-man team, consisting of 'Poncho' Alire, Bob Pegram, Richard Bellwood, Dan Bien and I dressed in camo fatigues. We wore our web gear with extra magazines, grenades, canteens of water and a couple of dehydrated meals. I wore the same camo cloth headband that I always wore on patrol. It covered my forehead, providing concealment, kept the sweat out of my eyes and didn't obstruct my peripheral vision the way a boonie cap did. I was still suffering a little from my fall from the speeding truck, but the contusions were healing nicely and the stiff muscles were resolving. However, the bruises still provided a constant reminder why man was not meant to fly.

We inserted at last light by US Navy riverine patrol boat. As the craft slowed and pulled into the shore, we jumped off onto the muddy bank and moved out in patrol formation approximately 150 meters before setting up in some thick cover for the rest of the night. The mosquitoes were horrible, making my turn on watch a miserable experience. The constant droning around my ears kept me wide awake, but swatting the swarming blood-suckers was a no-no. You just had to sit there and take it until your watch was over and you could lay back and cover your face with your headgear.

The next morning, during the false dawn, the entire team was alert, ready and waiting to move out. This was always the most dangerous time on patrol. It was the time when a hidden enemy force would often choose to strike. We sat motionless waiting for the true dawn to enable us to see what was going on around our position. Satisfied that we had not been observed and everything was as it should be, the team leader gave the signal to move out to the next checkpoint marked on our map.

The terrain consisted of thick jungle undergrowth with large numbers of banana, coconut and palm trees jutting up among the waist-high vegetation. Within the first 200 meters, we crossed several well-worn trails. We always avoided walking on them, preferring to parallel them a few meters back in the dense cover. Besides leaving unmistakable American footprints walking on the bare trails, the local VC would often booby-trap them if they suspected Americans were in the area.

Suddenly, as I passed under a large banana tree, a cluster of fire ants dropped from the foliage onto my head and neck. They immediately began biting with a viciousness that I had never experienced before. It was worse than being swarmed by honey bees. I started madly swatting at them, trying to drive them from my exposed flesh. As soon as my teammates realized that I had not gone insane or decided to do a horrible rendition of the Watusi out in the middle of the jungle, they grabbed their bottles of government-issue insect repellent and began spraying it on my head, neck and shoulders. Between the repellent and my frantic hand-slapping, I eventually managed to rid myself of these savage insects. The pain from the bites was almost unbearable. I wanted to scream out at the top of my lungs, but had to fight the urge so as not to alert anyone who happened to be nearby. After several minutes, the pain began to subside to the point where it was tolerable. I struggled to regulate my breathing, and when I finally got it under control, motioned to my teammates that I was ready to move on.

We continued patrolling slowly through the heavy cover, stopping occasionally to check our location with a map and compass, and to snack on a few bananas from one of the nearby trees.

Late in the afternoon the point man signaled for the team to hold up. Just ahead we could see what appeared to be a pagoda or some type of religious shrine set back in the dense vegetation. It was ancient and covered in vines and lush secondary growth. Inside the shrine was a weathered, carved stone Buddha. There was no sign in the immediate vicinity of the site that anyone had been there in ages. We marveled reverently at this sacred mystery in the middle of the jungle, then moved out again to find a secure site to set up a night defensive position.

A short time later, as dusk was setting in, we found a good spot back in the center of a thick patch of underbrush and set up an overnight hide site. We cleared the area of limbs and other debris and settled into a tight circle as the darkness fell over us. I pinched off a small piece of C-4 from a wad I carried in my pocket, filled my canteen cup with water and lit the thimble-sized ball of explosive which brought the water to a boil in seconds. Satisfied that it was hot enough to soften the beans in my chilli con carne dehydrated LRRP ration, I poured the contents of my cup into the plastic bag containing my meal, then set it aside for a few minutes while it rehydrated.

After we had finished eating and buried the plastic/cardboard containers, we settled head-to-head in a tight circle and, except for the team member designated to pull the first watch, quickly fell asleep.

The final morning of the patrol came too quickly. Before moving out to finish our mission, we discovered that our water supply was running dangerously low. We would have to be on the lookout for another source of water to refill our canteens. The heat and humidity would prove too much to bear without being able to replace the fluids we'd lose though perspiration.

Late in the morning we spotted a thatched hut about 20 meters to our front. We froze in position and observed it for the next ten to fifteen minutes. Satisfied that there was no one in the area, we moved up to the structure to check it out. We noticed a makeshift gutter, fashioned from a piece of plastic pipe, that ran along the edge of the thatched roof, then down into a large barrel that sat along the outer wall of the hut. Obviously, it served to catch and hold rainwater. It must have been effective because the barrel was full to overflowing. We took turns filling our canteens, placing a halazone tablet in each to kill any waterborne bacteria. The water purification tablets gave a mildly unpleasant taste to the water, but they were necessary if you didn't want to pick up any of the sicknesses lurking throughout the Vietnamese countryside. We made sure that we covered up any signs that we had been in the area, then moved out again for the next objective on our map.

Early in the afternoon we reached the edge of a large, open area dotted with mature palm trees. About 100 meters to our front, we spotted a hooch, standing alone in the middle of the clearing. Suddenly, a VC ran out of the structure and took off, sprinting to our left. Bob Pegram reacted quickly and dropped him with a well-aimed shot. The VC tumbled to the ground and rolled into a nearby depression. We eased up to where he had disappeared and found him lying dead at the bottom of shallow dry ravine.

While we were observing the body, four more Viet Cong broke from cover and darted to the right across a small clearing located between the palm forest and a banana grove on the far side. Before we had a chance to react, the enemy soldiers disappeared among the thick fruit trees.

The banana grove was not huge, perhaps 100 meters square, but the vegetation was thick enough that we knew it would be foolhardy to pursue the VC into it.

While we remained on high alert and observed the banana grove to make sure they didn't sneak out one side or the other, our team leader radioed for a pair of Cobra gunships. When they arrived on station a few minutes later, Alire requested them to hit the banana grove with everything they had. Immediately, all hell broke loose in front of us. The two gunships took turns expending their ordnance into the dense vegetation. Mini-guns, 40mm grenades and rockets tore the grove apart. We could feel the sharp concussion from the multiple rockets impacting among the trees and looked for a place to crawl into for cover, but there was nothing available.

When the Cobras had finished their deadly business, there wasn't a banana tree left standing in the grove. Smoke arose from numerous points and the vegetation looked as if Paul Bunyan had passed through it with a giant-size chain saw. I was truly amazed at the extent of the destruction. It was hard to believe that two helicopters could wreak that much damage in such a short period of time. It made me thankful that the enemy didn't have Cobra gunships. We knew that it would take a couple of hours crawling through that mess to determine if there were any enemy bodies in there and none of us really wanted to do that. We were satisfied that if the VC had remained in the banana grove, they were on their way to greet their ancestors.

We silently withdrew from the area and humped a few hundred meters to a suitable extraction point, arriving late in the afternoon. We quickly secured the pick-up zone and waited for the Huey that would arrive and take us back to our base camp at Dong Tam.

This was my first actual combat mission. I was satisfied with my performance, even though I had not fired a single round. There had been no fear or hesitation on my part, which filled in some of the questions I had asked myself. You never know ahead of time how you will respond on your first time in battle. You can only wait until it happens and trust that your character, your confidence and your training will take over and get you through it. It's been that way since the first two men decided to kill each other and it will likely continue until the last two men decide that peace is a better option. I was confident that I would perform well in future combat, and at the time, it made me feel extremely good about myself.

Chapter Six

On 10 October, we received an op order from G-2 for a mission laid on for that evening. We would be going onto the dreaded Thoi Son Island, nicknamed by 9th Division soldiers as 'VC Island'. In 1967 a battalion from the 9th Division swept the island, finding a few weapons and food caches, but taking heavy casualties from enemy snipers and hundreds of booby-traps. The Americans had paid a heavy price for their walk across the 7-mile-long island. They would never go back on it in force again. It wasn't worth the price. Later LRP missions had convinced us that the island was still well-stocked with numerous enemy troops who apparently didn't appreciate trespassers. The entire island was still laced with various intricate forms of booby-traps in large quantities. It was not a place one could drop his guard, even for a second. Movement there had to be slow and deliberate, and you had to be aware of everything within your line of sight. To let up, even for a second, was to invite injury or death. No one ever looked forward to a patrol on Thoi Son Island.

We were to be inserted that night by a US Navy patrol boat. As it was already late in the afternoon, Alire ordered us to get our gear ready and meet him at the Orderly Room for the trip out to the river. Just before dark, our three-quarter-ton truck dropped us off at the Navy's docking facility in the canal that ran out into the Mekong River. We climbed onto the waiting craft and took up positions wherever we could find an available space. I ended up near the stern for the fifteen-minute ride to our insertion point on the far end of the island.

As we neared the target area, I decided to move to the front of the boat to be closer to the bow when it touched the shore. I stepped up on the railing that ran around the perimeter of the patrol boat and grabbed onto the edge of the open pilot's station with my right hand for support. My weapon was in my left hand.

As I shifted my weight in anticipation of the boat touching the shore, a heavy volume of enemy fire erupted from the vegetation immediately to our front. We were still 30 meters from the shore line when the VC sprang their ambush. The boat commander threw the ship into reverse, which caused the prop wash to catch up to us and rock us hard in the water. At that same moment, a round from the VC buzzed past my left ear, leaving a small burn mark and causing a pressure imbalance that felt like air was being sucked out of my head. The close call from the bullet and the rocking motion from the patrol boat caused me to lose my balance, and the next thing I knew I was tumbling feet first into the dark waters of the Mekong River.

With the combined weight of my weapon, the radio, several magazines of ammo, two fragmentation grenades, a pair of smoke grenades, a concussion grenade and a canteen full of water, I knew that swimming to the surface was going to be something of a problem. As I sank quickly to the bottom of the river, a depth I guessed to be somewhere between 20 to 25ft, my first thought was to drop everything I had on me and swim for the shore, but realizing what would be waiting for me there made me hesitate about shedding my weapon and equipment. I sensed that if I didn't do something quickly, the current would carry me downstream and that would be the end of Jimmy Thayer. Although everything was pitch black, I could tell from the force of the current and the way I had entered the river that the shoreline had to be directly to my front. I took off, bouncing along the bottom in that direction as fast as I could. In seconds, I felt the river bed rising slowly in front of me. I began using the butt of my rifle as a lever, digging it into the mud bottom ahead of me, then pulling it back to keep my momentum moving forward. My remaining oxygen was rapidly escaping through my lips and bubbling toward the surface. My lungs were screaming for a new source of air. Somewhere in the deep recesses of my brain, I knew I was about to drown.

Suddenly, my head broke the surface of the river. I could hear myself gasping and sucking for air. Tracers were crisscrossing in the black night above me. Somewhere off in the distance behind me, I heard my teammates on the boat yelling: 'THERE HE IS…THERE HE IS!'

The powerful motors of the patrol boat kicked into gear as it surged toward me. Still trying to orient myself in the darkness, I turned around to face the oncoming PBR. I was totally unprepared when the prow of the boat rammed hard into my chest, smashing me back into the muddy riverbank. Alire began shouting: 'GODDAMN, YOU HIT HIM…BACK UP, BACK UP.'

The boat reversed direction away from the shoreline, ground to a stop, then plowed forward again, hitting me a second time and driving me even deeper into the muddy embankment. I kept struggling, fighting the suction of the mud and trying to figure out why the PBR was trying to kill me. Finally, I managed to free myself from the sticky gumbo, but the exertion had left me pretty well drained of my last reserves of energy. I was confused, weak and almost totally helpless, standing there knee-deep in the dark water wondering what was going to happen next. Once again, the boat reversed away from the riverbank, backing out 30 meters into the channel.

In the darkness, I heard Pegram yell directions for the boat commander to move to the right as he headed back in a third time. As the craft pulled into the shore 5ft from where I stood, dripping mud into the water, I had just enough energy left to make a final lunge for the side of the boat. My teammates were there to reach down, grab me and the radio and yank me up onto the bow of the patrol boat. Finally out of the river, I could manage only to lay there helplessly on the deck, gasping like a beached whale with my head resting upon the radio. I didn't move as the boat once again backed away from the shore, then turned and sped upstream in the direction of Dong Tam.

Our mission had been compromised during the insertion attempt. The VC had heard the boat coming and had set up a hasty ambush, but in the dark of the night they had initiated it a little too soon. Their mistake had saved our lives. Once again, luck had been on our side.

Chapter Seven

On 12 October I was sitting on my bunk cleaning my M16 when Richard Bellwood came over, sat down next to me, and said: 'Hey, Jim, do you remember last week when I rode down to Tan An with the Sergeant to drop off the mail, and we stopped at My Tho and had a beer with some girls at a bar?' I nodded and continued wiping the oil onto the metal surfaces of my weapon. 'Well, I met one that I really liked. She was pretty and very nice to me,' he muttered rather sheepishly. I nodded and replied: 'That's cool.' 'Well, I want to go back and see her again,' he said, almost apologetically. 'Okay,' I answered, 'we'll go in the morning if we don't have a mission.' 'How are we going to get there?' Bellwood enquired. I said: 'Why, Richard, we'll go by river.'

The next morning came and when I found out that we were still on stand-down, I told Bellwood: 'Okay, let's go find a Navy patrol boat and hitch a ride down the river to My Tho.' We hurried down to the Navy dock where the boats were berthed and asked a few of the sailors if anyone was going downstream. One of them looked up and said: 'Yeah, we are.' I asked him if he minded if we hitched a ride to My Tho. He smiled and said: 'Of course not, come aboard.'

Twenty minutes later the patrol boat pulled into the community dock at My Tho. I thanked the boat crew as Bellwood and I jumped ashore and headed for the bar in the center of town. When we arrived there, a pretty young girl came running over to Richie and gave him a big hug. Bellwood introduced her to me, saying her name was 'Lin'. I told her to call me Jim and the three of us sat down at a nearby table. I ordered a couple of beers for us and a Saigon tea for Lin. I was surprised to discover that she spoke enough basic English for us to manage to carry on a fairly intelligent conversation. Richie seemed to be pleased that I appeared to be enjoying myself. Thirty minutes later, he leaned across the table and whispered to me that she had a room across the street at the hotel and wanted him to go there with her. I smiled and said: 'That's cool, let's go.' He laughed, shook his head and answered: 'No, you don't understand. Not you…just me!' I grinned at his obvious embarrassment and replied: 'I know that, Richie. I'll just wait outside in the hall.'

We hurriedly finished our beers and left the bar, heading for the hotel across the street. We entered the dusty lobby and made for the stairwell heading up to the second floor where Lin's room was located. As Richie and his girl entered the room and closed the door quietly behind them, I found a spot at the top of the stairs where I could observe both her room and the stairway down to the first floor. I took a seat on the top step, my CAR-15 across my lap.

About ten minutes had passed when I heard three loud explosions outside in the street between the hotel and the bar, followed immediately by a burst of heavy automatic gunfire. Seconds later, two Vietnamese men ran to the bottom of the stairs and looked up, surprised to see me sitting on the top step. One of them said in broken English: 'You go now. VC come soon.' I pointed my weapon at him and shouted: 'No. You go.' They looked at each other, then took off, running toward the front door of the hotel.

The city of My Tho was under attack, and here I was guarding my teammate who was, at that moment, busily engaged in unknown carnal pleasures with a Vietnamese hooker just down the hall. There was nowhere to go, so I made up my mind that if any VC showed up and tried to come up the stairs, I would sure as hell blow them away. I could have kicked myself in the butt for not having the foresight to have brought along another beer or two with me when we left the bar. Then my better judgment kicked in. Realizing the danger our current situation presented, I jumped to my feet and yelled down the hall for Richie to get his clothes on and get the hell out here. We needed to go; the Viet Cong were attacking the city. Richie shouted back: 'Okay, okay…in just a few minutes.' At that point, I was more concerned about getting caught outside our base camp than running into the VC.

Finally, Bellwood came out of the room buttoning up his shirt and asked me: 'What are we going to do?' I said: 'Slide a round in your chamber and we'll wait and see what's going on. And ask Lin if she has any cold beer in her fridge.'

Thirty minutes later the shooting stopped, and we decided to make our way back to the dock. The attack was over, the VC had left the city and the 'all clear' sirens began to whine. As we were making our way toward the dock, an Army deuce and a half truck came roaring down the street behind us. I stepped out in the oncoming lane and flagged down the driver. When he screeched to a stop 10ft in front of me, I walked around to the driver's side and asked him if he was headed to Dong Tam. He nodded and told us to hop in the back. I'm sure after the recent attack on the city he was happy to have a couple of armed GIs pulling security for him.

When we arrived back at our company area, we told our teammates about our recent misadventure in My Tho. They laughed and commented on how lucky we had been not to have been killed by the VC or arrested by the MPs on our return. I told them we were indeed fortunate to have avoided both outcomes. I hastily added that if you didn't take a chance now and then, you'd just never have any fun.

Chapter Eight

A few days later, on 15 October, we received orders for a quick in-and-out mission several klicks (kilometers) out from Dong Tam on the Mekong River. The team consisted of Alire, Pegram, DeLeon, Myers, Charles Hendrickson, Richard Bellwood and me. Alire told us we'd be going in 'light' and would be inserted by Navy patrol boat.

When we reached the Navy docking facilities on the canal in Dong Tam, we climbed aboard the boat and headed out to the river. The patrol boat moved into the main channel and roared off downstream past VC Island and the town of My Tho. The PBR finally reached a point on the opposite shore, 400 meters from a small village that was set back away from the river. Alire told the Chief Petty Officer in charge of the patrol boat to stand off in a canal we had passed on the way to our insertion point. He nodded that he understood, and we quickly leaped to the shore and headed south through the heavy cover that ran along the river.

After 'playing ghost' for a few minutes to make sure that we hadn't attracted any attention coming ashore, we turned and moved quietly in the direction of the village. Thirty minutes later, we reached the outskirts of the small hamlet and set up an OP (observation point) to monitor the activity in and around the village. We were looking for armed VC or NVA, but anything suspicious or out of the ordinary would surely be of interest to us.

There was the usual activity one would expect to find around a small Vietnamese village. People were coming and going constantly, several working in the nearby rice paddies, others doing chores and odd jobs. Some children were playing games and shouting back and forth to each other, while others were herding a flock of ducks away from one of the rice paddies.

Suddenly, we spotted three VC approaching the village from the east. They were armed, walking in single file, nonchalantly talking back and forth to each other. It was obvious that they never suspected they were being watched by an American long-range reconnaissance patrol. When they reached the village, they stopped at the first hooch and set their weapons against the outer wall of the building. Now unarmed, they approached a frail, elderly man squatting on the ground in front of a fire pit, then sat down across from him with their backs toward the hooch. The Vietnamese elder appeared to be brewing tea in a metal pot hanging over the coals. He lifted the pot and began pouring tea into some tin cups stacked next to him on the ground. The VC nodded their thanks as they accepted the tea from the white-haired old man. The three enemy soldiers were dressed alike in white shirts and black shorts. They were wearing the usual Ho Chi Minh sandals on their feet. We realized that they were probably local VC who lived in the village. The men seemed remarkably relaxed and unaware of the danger they were in.

We whispered among ourselves that we should try to capture them. In full agreement, we came up with a quick plan to accomplish the task. We decided to split up into two groups with Alire, Bellwood, Myers and me moving in from the right side of the building. Pegram, Hendrickson and DeLeon would come in from the left side. Getting into position without being seen would prove to be a challenge, but the opportunity to capture three POWs was well worth the risk.

Keeping the hooch between us and the four Vietnamese peacefully drinking their tea, we moved into position directly behind the building. Alire whispered that we would make our play in one minute. Everyone nodded, then we split into our separate groups and moved up along the opposite sides of the hooch.

At the given moment, we came charging around the front corners of the hooch, screaming for the VC to get down on the ground. I'm certain that they had no idea what we were shouting at them, but the intensity of our actions and the tone of our voices encouraged them to do exactly as we wanted. We had them trapped between our two elements and there was no way for them to flee or reach their weapons.

The three enemy soldiers raised their hands, then quickly dropped to the ground. The old man remained seated with his mouth agape, searching for words that wouldn't come. He appeared to be so terrified that we thought for sure he was having a stroke.

Three of my teammates secured the prisoners, while two others kept their weapons trained on them. Alire grabbed the handset on my radio and called for the patrol boat waiting upstream. He told the Chief that he had three POWs and instructed him to meet us in twenty minutes at the riverbank nearest the village.

Hendrickson and I escorted the prisoners back to the boat, while the remainder of the team searched the huts in the hamlet. Myers grabbed the VC weapons still leaning against the outer wall of the hooch. Two were AK-47s and one was an SKS semi-automatic carbine.

Twenty minutes later, as Hendrickson and I were nearing the riverbank with the prisoners, the rest of the team caught up to us. The patrol boat was there, idling 30 meters out in the river. When the Chief saw us move out on the muddy riverbank, he kicked the boat into gear and pulled into the shore. The crew helped us load the prisoners and the captured weapons on board. Then the team settled in for the thirty-minute ride back to Dong Tam where we turned over our captives to Division G-2 personnel for interrogation.

It was a great coup for us. Capturing three armed VC soldiers without taking any casualties was quite an accomplishment. We were beaming like a bunch of high-school football players after winning the state championship when we reached the company area. Tango 1-1 had indeed earned some bragging rights for the successful mission, and we planned on exercising those rights at our club that evening.

Chapter Nine

On 3 November G-3 (Division Operations) decided it was time to send another patrol onto Thoi Son Island in the middle of the Mekong River. No one had been to the dreaded 'VC Island' since my team, Tango 1-1, had been shot at on insertion back on 10 October. C.R. Mathis' team got the nod for the mission this time. They were to be inserted at first light on the morning of the 4th by riverine patrol boat.

Just before daylight on the day of the mission, the team boarded the PBR at the Navy docks and motored out to the river before heading downstream toward their insertion point on the lower end of the island. Their landing was uncontested, so the team moved quickly into the dense underbrush and 'went ghost' for nearly twenty minutes to make sure their insertion had not been observed. Satisfied that they had not been spotted, the team moved out toward the interior of the island.

Sometime just before midday they reached a point nearly a mile from the river where they stumbled upon several camouflaged huts spread out in some thick underbrush, surrounded by a stand of mature bamboo. The huts were well-hidden and almost impossible to spot from the air.

The team remained in hiding and watched the structures for nearly fifteen minutes. Finally deciding that they were unoccupied, the LRPs moved in cautiously to search the area for anything that might be of value to the Intel people at Division G-2. It wasn't long before they uncovered a weapons cache and a large supply of rice inside two of the structures. There were also some cooking pots and pans and a couple of sleeping mats that indicated someone had been using the site. Deciding not to touch anything, the five LRPs backed off into the surrounding cover and called in their discovery to their commanding officer back at Dong Tam.

Suddenly, a long burst of AK-47 fire erupted from a patch of dense cover on the back side of the huts. The team leader, still holding the radio

34

handset, was hit in the buttocks by a single round. The bullet traveled down through his leg and exited out of his knee. It was a serious wound that required an immediate medevac.

No one had seen where the gunfire had come from. While one of the team members began treating the wounded team leader, the remainder of the LRPs desperately scoped out the surrounding area trying to locate the enemy sniper who had fired them up. They realized that they had to get the wounded man extracted and decided that the fastest way was to carry him back to the river. While three team members left with the casualty, Mathis remained behind to make sure they weren't followed. He secretly hoped that the hidden VC might think the entire team had pulled out and step out into the open and show himself. Mathis waited ten minutes and when nothing happened, slipped silently away to catch up with his teammates.

It was mid-afternoon when they reached the shoreline. The PBR boat was waiting for them. The crew helped them get their casualty aboard and then quickly transported the team back to Dong Tam. After seeing to it that their wounded team leader was on his way to a surgical ward at Ton San Nhut, they reported what they had found to a staff officer at Division G-3. The debriefing officer listened intently to what the LRPs had to say, then asked them to wait while he conferred with his senior officers. He returned a short time later and told the team that he wanted them to go back to the island and lead an infantry platoon to the cache site.

Thirty minutes later, the LRPs were once again on the PBR headed back to VC Island. They reached shore 100 meters upstream from their previous landing site, hoping to avoid an ambush. Just behind them, a flat-bowed ATC (Armored Troop Carrier) pulled into shore, lowered its ramp, and dropped off a reinforced infantry platoon. The waiting LRPs linked up with the line unit, then waited while the team's ATL told the lieutenant in command of the infantry that his team would take point and lead him and his platoon back to the cache site, a little over a klick inland.

Forty minutes later, the LRPs pulled up at the edge of the underbrush where the hooches were located and signaled for the infantry to move up on-line. There was still plenty of daylight left, but the ATL wanted to get the mission over with and get back to Dong Tam before dark. He wanted to find out how his wounded team leader was doing. As the infantry maneuvered to approach the first hooch, VC soldiers hidden in the dense cover behind the buildings sprang their ambush on both the LRPs and the infantry platoon. The Americans returned fire as they dove for cover.

The infantry unit had taken several casualties in the opening moments of the ambush. Three Americans were killed outright and several others were wounded. Among the LRPs, Mathis had taken a round in his bicep and another LRP, Ron Moore, was shot in the abdomen. He died a few moments later.

As the battle raged around them, the two unwounded LRPs pulled their dead teammate back from where he had fallen. Mathis crawled over to join them. They discussed the situation among themselves and decided to get Moore's body back to the shoreline. They had completed their mission by leading the infantry platoon to the cache site. It had cost them two more casualties. The infantry platoon could handle the ongoing battle. LRPs were not trained for extended firefights.

Two of the LRPs moved out, carrying Moore's body between them. Mathis dropped behind to pull rear security for his teammates as they struggled back to the river with their load. The infantry remained at the initial point of contact, still heavily engaged with the hidden enemy. Both sides would suffer additional casualties before the battle ended later in the afternoon with the VC finally withdrawing.

The LRPs were extracted back to Dong Tam where Moore's body was turned over to Graves Registration. Mathis was treated at the med center in Dong Tam, then medevacked to military hospital at Tan Son Nhut. The next day he was airlifted to Camp Zama in Japan. A month later, he was flown to the military hospital at Fort Lewis, Washington where he spent four more months going through additional surgeries and physical therapy. He was awarded a Bronze Star with 'V' device for his actions that day in November and unceremoniously given a medical retirement from the military. His war was over.

Chapter Ten

On 6 November Division G-3 sent word to our commanding officer to combine a pair of five-man teams into a ten-man hunter/killer patrol for a mission into a pre-designated area not far from the 9th Infantry Division's base camp at Dong Tam. The mission was to search out and destroy an enemy force known to be operating in that area. Division G-2 had received reliable Intel from two different agents that the VC were there now. Team Tango 1-1 was one of the two teams selected for the patrol.

'Poncho' Alire was no longer Tango 1-1's TL. He had recently taken over the position of Operations NCO at the LRP Company Tactical Operations Center (TOC). His job entailed running all missions out of Dong Tam and Tan An. Bob Pegram had been given command of the team and I had been appointed his assistant team leader (ATL). Richard Bellwood, Dan Bien and Mike O'Day made up the rest of the team. The TL of the other team selected for the mission was given the overall command of the combined 'heavy' team for the patrol.

We were inserted later in the day by a pair of Huey slicks. As usual, the first Huey banked and dropped down toward our LZ. The first two LRPs quickly slid out of the open cabin and onto the skid. When the aircraft was within 3 to 4ft from the ground, the two men jumped, followed by the next two, then finally the last man on the team. The surface of the ground dictated the height. The chopper never came to a hover, and when the door-gunner signaled that the last man was out, the pilot lifted back to altitude, continuing his flight path. The second Huey followed suit and soon all ten of us were on the ground.

The helicopters had dropped us into an open area between a pair of hooches and a dry rice paddy. There was a large section of woods flanking the far side of the rice paddy 150 meters away. We could make out a wide grassy strip bordering the trees out to the edge of the field.

Another narrow tree-line to our right ran across one end of the rice paddy and intersected with the larger forest on the other side. There was a dense patch of underbrush between the hooches and the open area where the choppers had inserted us.

We moved quickly into patrol formation and prepared to move out. Jim Martens, the point man for the other team, moved into the lead position, with his team leader falling in behind him to walk his 'slack'. Bob Pegram, my TL, took up the third slot with the senior RTO directly behind him. I settled into the #5 position and the rest of the patrol fell in behind me. The team leader gave the signal to move out, indicating that Martens was to head across a paddy dike toward the woods on the far side of the rice paddy. I thought to myself that this was not a good thing, to be moving across this wide, open area. There was no cover and concealment on the paddy dike, and if the enemy caught us there, we'd literally be between a rock and a hard place. I whispered my doubts to Pegram walking to my immediate front, only to have him whisper back that the other team leader was in charge.

We made it across the paddy dike and moved into the grassy strip bordering the wood-line, then turned and walked down the strip flanking the trees. At that point the palm forest was wide enough that we couldn't see what was on the other side of it. We had covered about 30 meters when several hidden enemy soldiers suddenly opened fire on us at very close range from back in the cover of the trees. Out of my peripheral vision I saw our point man take a round in the knee and collapse heavily to the ground.

We countered the ambush by turning toward the tree-line and emptying our weapons on fully-automatic into the forest to establish fire superiority over the enemy forces concealed there. I couldn't say for certain if we killed anyone or not, but the subsequent enemy fire was not as heavy nor very accurate.

As I shoved a fresh magazine into my weapon, I noticed that the team leader had grabbed the wounded point man by the leg and was trying to pull him back from the edge of the woods. I ran over to him and yelled: 'I've got him.' I picked up Martens in my arms and carried him 30 meters back through the grassy area we had just traversed.

The team leader, along with most of the team, turned and ran for the cover of the huts on the far side of the paddy. When they reached the structures, they quickly took up positions in the brush between the hooches and the edge of the paddy and began firing across the open field into the wood-line to give Pegram, Martens and I the chance to withdraw out of the kill zone to safety.

With Pegram at my side, we stopped at the edge of the rice paddy where a dike crossed the field. I lifted Martens onto Pegram's back and shouted for him to keep going. I would stay behind and cover them. As Pegram lumbered across the paddy dike carrying Martens piggy-back-style, I grabbed both their weapons and began returning fire into the enemy positions as I continued to withdraw behind them. To this day I don't know how we made it back to the rest of the team without being hit. Enemy rounds kicked up dust all around me and chased after Pegram and Martens as they fled.

When we reached the questionable safety of the huts and rejoined our teammates, we dressed Martens' wound and called for a medevac. The battle continued, with both sides exchanging rounds across the open paddy. Within minutes, the helicopter, bearing a large red cross on its nose, flared to a hard landing outside one of the huts. With rounds impacting all around us, we hustled Martens on board and shouted to the pilot to get the hell out of there.

While we were extracting our wounded point man, an enemy round had passed through the wall of one of the huts. Bob Pegram and I heard the frantic screaming of a female coming from the hut and hurried over to find a middle-aged Vietnamese woman hovering over the body of a young boy about 13 to 14 years old. He had been shot in the head and was bleeding profusely. Although the wound looked serious, the boy was still conscious. We tried to comfort the mother while putting a pressure dressing on her wounded son. The team leader called for another medevac, telling the radio relay team to have it land on our smoke when it reached our location.

When we finally heard the approaching Huey, one of the LRPs popped a yellow smoke grenade and tossed it into the clearing behind the huts. This enabled the medevac to touch down outside the vision of the VC who were still firing from the wood-line on the far side of the paddy. We hurriedly loaded both the wounded boy and his mother into the Huey and gave a 'thumbs-up' to the pilot.

The enemy fire died down immediately after the second aircraft left the area. We whispered among ourselves that the enemy must have thought that we had been extracted in the two aircraft. Silently, we spread out in the brush directly in front of the hooches and waited to see what would happen next.

A few minutes later, five armed VC stepped out of the tree-line and began searching the grassy strip where they had first ambushed our team. This time it was their turn to be surprised. Nine LRPs opened fire simultaneously and our mission was accomplished. Satisfied that none of the VC survived, we regrouped and called for an extraction. Our team leader had decided that it would be too dangerous to cross the paddy to check the bodies and recover their weapons. We had no idea if there were additional enemy forces still hidden in the woods.

We later discovered that Jim Martens, our wounded point man, had been airlifted to Japan, then back to the States for a long rehab. He was our fourth casualty in two days. The 9th Division LRPs had lost one man killed in action and three more out of the war for good. It was a tough time for us all.

Chapter Eleven

As December approached, E Company, 50th Infantry (LRP) was running missions not only out of the 1st Brigade AO at Dong Tam, but also out of Fire Base Moore (south-west of Saigon in the Mekong Delta), for the 2nd Brigade off the USS *Benewah* anchored in the Mekong River, and in the 3rd Brigade AO at Tan An. Many of our missions involved running recon patrols for infantry units, a job we didn't much care for. It was a job normally reserved for battalion recon elements, not for LRPs. Too many times while scouting ahead of infantry operations we found ourselves stuck in the middle between the infantry and the enemy, being shot at by both sides.

One night in November when Richard Bellwood, Mike O'Day and I went on a recon patrol for an infantry company we soon found ourselves in the middle of a prolonged firefight between some GIs and a squad of VC. It was raining 'cats and dogs' while the battle raged around us, so the three of us took shelter in a muddy bomb crater to avoid the tracer rounds passing back and forth just above our heads. After several hours, the heavy rains caused the water level in our subterranean shelter to rise to life-threatening levels. The three of us slipped out of the flooded bomb crater in the middle of the night and low-crawled across a muddy field into the nearby jungle to find sanctuary under some sturdy banana trees.

Early the next morning, after the battle and the rain had ended, we counted our blessings and thanked the gods that none of us had caught a stray round during the firefight the previous night. We were cold, wet and miserable and decided it was a good time to move to a better location. It was at that moment we spotted five Viet Cong approaching us from the north. We waited a few minutes hoping they would change direction, but they seemed intent on seeking shelter in the same wood-line we had just decided to vacate. We had no choice but to engage the enemy because they would have walked dead into our position if we had waited much longer. A nasty firefight ensued. While our little battle raged, one of the VC managed to get close enough to attempt to toss a Chicom grenade into our position. Fortunately for us, he was shot as he was about to throw the frag and it fell short of reaching us before it went off. However, a small piece of shrapnel from the resulting explosion did manage to embed itself in my solar plexus about 3in below my sternum. It was not a serious wound, a tiny piece of metal lodging just beneath the skin.

The firefight ended quickly in our favor, so we high-tailed it as quickly as we could back to our base camp. After reporting our action to the Intel people, I climbed up on a bunker and dug out the shrapnel with the tip of my K-Bar combat knife. Satisfied that the job was done but knowing that my future as a surgeon left a lot to be desired, I went to see the infantry company medic to get some antibiotic salve to fight any infection that might occur. He gave me a tube of some type of white cream and told me to keep the wound clean and covered with this ointment. I thought: 'Yeah, like how in the hell do I keep the wound clean in Vietnam?'

Well, the wound ended up getting infected anyway and began to drain pus and fluids constantly. It took two more trips to see the medic, constant applications of the antibiotic cream and occasional peroxide rinses over the next three weeks for it to fully heal. It was difficult for me to accept the fact that such a tiny wound could cause so much trouble.

Chapter Twelve

For a brief time in late November, I pulled a few missions while operating off the USS *Benewah*. The *Benewah* was a US Navy berthing ship. The ship spent most of 1968–69 anchored in the Mekong River. In addition to serving as a berthing ship, the *Benewah* also provided medical facilities, quartermaster stores, headquarters and other services for the sailors and the 2nd Brigade soldiers operating with the Mobile Riverine Force.

The *Benewah* was frequently the target of enemy attacks, and her guns were called upon to defend her on numerous occasions. The soldiers and sailors fortunate enough to operate out of this massive floating base camp experienced clean and sanitary facilities, excellent food, hot showers and a well-stocked canteen, all features virtually unknown to the average combat soldier in Vietnam.

In the middle of November, my team had been assigned to the *Benewah* for three weeks running missions with the Navy PBR boats. It was great sleeping in the stacked bunks on comfortable mattresses and clean sheets. The food in the Navy mess hall was restaurant quality, cooked to taste and served in quantity and variety that my teammates and I were not used to. We LRPs thought we had indeed died and gone to heaven.

One of our first missions was an insertion by PBR boat near a tiny hamlet surrounded by numerous rice paddies. After landing on the shoreline, we quickly moved inland and set up an OP in a narrow tree-line just outside the village. We had observed the area for nearly an hour when we spotted ten armed VC moving across one of the paddies toward the hamlet.

The enemy seemed unaware of the LRP team watching them from less than 100 meters away. It was too good an opportunity to pass up. Without hesitation, we initiated contact and engaged the VC with small-arms fire, forcing them to seek what shelter they could find in the rice paddy. While my teammates were putting rounds down range, I got on the radio, called a nearby artillery unit and requested a fire mission.

I asked for a smoke round at coordinates 100ft directly to our front. It was a little close for artillery, but my plan was to walk the shells into the enemy. Less than a minute later we heard the incoming round whining overhead as it neared the target site.

Instead of bursting 100ft out in the rice paddy like I had planned, the round hit one of the nearby hooches, setting it aflame. As the thatched hut began to burn to the ground, two more VC burst through the door and sprinted for the nearest rice paddy. We opened fire, cutting them down before they had covered 10 meters.

I got back on the radio and shouted: 'FIRE FOR EFFECT.' In seconds HE rounds began exploding among the huts and out in the paddy where the surviving VC were trying to flee. After several salvos had blanketed the area, it was over. I called for a cease-fire and thanked the 'red-legs' for their great work. It always paid dividends to let your support people know that they were effective and much appreciated.

We backed away from the scene of the carnage and moved back to the river to meet up with our patrol boat. On the run back down the river to the *Benewah* Bellwood told me that his M16 had jammed during the firefight. He had a round locked up in the chamber. I told him to wait until we got back to the ship and I would work on it to remove the round.

Finally, back aboard the ship, we were walking down a flight of stairs toward the sleeping area that had been assigned to us below deck. Bellwood took that opportunity to pull the slide back on his weapon and let it fly forward again. In the enclosed passageway, the noise of the round going off was deafening, as was the sound of the 5.56mm bullet ricocheting off the steel walls on both sides of the gangway. Sailors and soldiers alike dove for whatever cover they could find. Only the two of us knew for sure whether it was an accidental discharge or the first shot of an enemy assault.

I looked at Bellwood and muttered under my breath: 'Damn, Richie, I told you I would work on it. Don't say a word.' Richie could be pretty laid back at times, and only shrugged his shoulders, grinning sheepishly. About that time a Navy ensign came running down the stairs. 'What was that?' he demanded. 'What was what, Sir?' I responded. 'You know what…that shot,' he growled, getting madder by the minute. 'Shot, Sir? I didn't hear anything. Did any of you guys hear a shot?' I asked, looking around at the crowd gathering at the bottom of the stairs. No one admitted to anything, and the frustrated young officer shook his head and finally turned to go back up the stairs. It took several minutes for the laughter to subside. I pointed toward Richie and cocked my eyebrows. He smiled back at me.

Chapter Thirteen

LRPs were not sent on missions during their final month in-country. It was Company policy. Tango 1-1 had just lost a pair of very experienced leaders in a very short time. I was given the position of team leader of Tango 1-1. I knew that I would have to step up quickly and get a few successful missions under my belt in order to gain the confidence and know-how that Alire and Pegram had brought to the team. I only hoped that I would be up to the task.

I appointed O'Day to serve as my ATL. He was the most experienced man on my team and had shown that he could take charge if something happened to me. I named Laure as my Senior RTO. Bellwood also remained with the team. He had been walking drag on a few missions, but I would also use him occasionally to hump the back-up radio.

Our team was sent to Tan An, headquarters of the 3rd Brigade of the 9th Infantry Division. We would miss the *Benewah* and all the fringe benefits that went with a tour there, but looked forward to the new assignment in the 3rd Brigade AO.

The 3rd Brigade compound at Tan An was located just outside the city of Tan An. The LRPs had their own area inside the base camp with a single-story barracks and an operations shed. There was no supply room and the officer in charge slept in the same barracks with the ranks. We kept our extra ammo, frags, Claymores (mines) and weapons with us in our barracks. There was a mess hall nearby which made it convenient for us to eat out for a change. We would not have to rely on LRP rations and foodstuffs sent from home while stationed at Tan An. The base was enclosed by concentric rings of barbed, concertina and razor wire. Fighting positions and bunkers were located back inside the wire. Most were constructed of 50-gallon drums filled with dirt and reinforced by layers of sandbags stacked across the top. Heavily-protected elevated guard towers were erected at various points around the base. There were established fields of fire all along the outer perimeter, and in case of an enemy ground assault, all personnel were assigned to defend designated positions along the perimeter. There was also a small helipad near our barracks that was designated as our departure point for missions out in the surrounding countryside.

We couldn't help but notice that MPs were stationed at the main gate which meant that there would be no free access into the city of Tan An. We didn't know at the time if the city was off limits or not, but it was something we would have to deal with if it was. It would be considered cruel and unusual punishment to build a base camp next to a large city and then deprive the occupants of that base camp the opportunity to partake in the carnal pleasures available there. LRPs wouldn't stand for such mistreatment.

Chapter Fourteen

When we arrived at Tan An, we discovered that the OIC (Officer in Charge) of the LRP element stationed there had just come in from the field where he had led a team on a very successful mission. First Lieutenant Robert Hill had transferred into the unit a couple of weeks earlier from a line company. He was an experienced combat leader who preferred leading from the front and demonstrated it by immediately volunteering to join teams on their missions. While waiting to report to him, one of the LRPs who accompanied him on the patrol gave us the details of this latest operation. He said that the team, led by Lieutenant Hill, had gone in at last light on 30 November. They had set up in a depression behind two intersecting dikes overlooking a football field-sized rice paddy. Early the next morning, they spotted an individual walking toward their position. Since the man was unarmed, they allowed him to approach. When he was within 50ft of the team, he put his hands out in front of him and began shouting '*Chieu Hoi...Chieu Hoi*', which was the US/RVN-inspired program that allowed enemy soldiers to switch sides and join up with the Allied Forces. When the man reached their perimeter, two of the LRPs grabbed him and pulled him down, tying his hands behind his back and gagging him. He might have been a willing '*Chieu Hoi*', but the LRPs weren't about to take his word for it. They would let Operations back at Tan An establish his bona fides. Lieutenant Hill radioed for a slick to come out to the team's location to evacuate the man.

When the aircraft landed nearby a short time later, the team took him out and placed him aboard for the short flight back to S-2 (Brigade Intelligence) back at Tan An. The team then relocated to a new location and set up again in a thicket at the end of a tree-line overlooking an open field. About 100 meters across the open area, another tree-line ran down the entire length of the field. At 1030 hours, the LRPs saw an armed VC step out of the tree-line, turn left and begin walking along the edge of the field. When he reached the end, he turned right and began walking directly toward the team's hide site. Hill signaled for his teammates to wait until he got closer, and at 75ft he and Sergeant Rick Ehrler each fired a single shot, killing the VC instantly.

The LRPs waited for nearly ten minutes to make sure that the VC hadn't been the point element for a larger enemy unit. Satisfied that the man had been alone, Lieutenant Hill and Specialist Fourth Class Richard Bellwood slipped cautiously out into the open field to search the body. They returned a short time later with an AK-47 assault rifle, a set of web gear, a handful of documents and a military ID card, and a Zenith AM/FM radio in a homemade case that the enemy soldier had been carrying over his shoulder.

Hill reported the contact to their radio relay team, then relocated once again to a new position where they set up another OP to cover a series of paddy dikes. After an uneventful night, the team was extracted at first light the next morning.

When we finally got to meet Lieutenant Hill, we were immediately impressed with the man. Not only was he a natural leader, he was also friendly and an easy man to talk to. There was none of the arrogance and sense of superiority that plagued many young officers in Vietnam. For the first time, I began to appreciate Captain Dickey's decision to send Tango 1-1 to Tan An.

Chapter Fifteen

At mid-morning on 3 December, Lieutenant Hill came into our barracks to inform us that he had just gotten word that there would be a USO show in the 3rd Brigade briefing room at 1500 hours. The large building was not far from our platoon area, so several of us decided that we would go there and catch the performance. It had been a long time since we had a chance for a little levity. The occasional outdoor movies at Dong Tam had been a poor substitute for live entertainment.

We arrived early and placed our berets on the first fifteen chairs on the right side of the seating area nearest the entry point. A small stage had been erected at the back of the building and approximately sixty chairs had been set up facing the stage. There were six rows of ten chairs divided down the middle by a narrow aisle. We didn't hang around to wait for the show to start, but felt confident that no one would dishonor us by moving our berets off the seats we had saved.

Just before 1500 hours, the building began to fill up fast with 3rd Brigade personnel arriving from all over the base camp. When the show finally started, I was sitting in the front row with four of my teammates, with ten more LRPs occupying the two rows behind us. We were elated to discover that the show was an all-female revue complete with singers, dancers and even a magician.

Early in the performance, the magician, a very lovely and well-endowed young lady, stepped down from the stage and began looking over the seated soldiers. Suddenly, she looked directly at me and asked if I would mind joining her on stage to serve as her assistant. Since she was a dead ringer for the luscious Ann Margret, I was all too happy to accede to her request. It turned out that she required my help with an illusion and a couple of card tricks. I obeyed like a trained dog, my eyes locked on this vision of loveliness. When her performance finally came to an end, she thanked me and gave me a big hug which nearly caused me to swallow my tongue. As I stepped from the stage to rejoin my fellow LRPs, they joined in with the rest of the crowd to give me a standing ovation. I can't say I remember much of anything that happened afterwards.

The larger USO shows were held at the Division base camp at Dong Tam. The mini-shows went out from Dong Tam to perform at the smaller base camps and some of the fire bases. Although the shows were infrequent, they were always well-attended by the soldiers fortunate enough to be able to see them. They provided a welcome interlude from the war, and for a couple of hours, an opportunity to see some attractive young ladies from the USA. It was a reminder of what we had left behind, and a promise of what we had to look forward to if we survived the war. For too many, it would be a promise that would go unfulfilled.

Chapter Sixteen

On 15 December, I packed my bags and signed out of the company for an R&R (Rest and Recreation) to Hawaii. I had looked forward to it for a couple of months. I had even been sending home the bulk of my pay to cover the cost for my wife and baby daughter to meet me there. Now the moment had arrived. I would soon be able to spend a full week with my family.

When my flight landed in Honolulu, things didn't go well for me at all. I sensed something was wrong as soon as my wife met me at the airport. She had never been cold to me before, but this time there was no feeling, no emotion, no anything when I walked up and tried to embrace her, and later, back at the hotel, she barely spoke to me. During the time we spent together that week, there was never any intimacy and little conversation. It proved to be nothing but an ordeal for us both. We slept in separate beds and there was no interest in or opportunity for love-making. By the end of the week, I wasn't even sure why she had agreed to come to Hawaii to meet me. However, it was wonderful to see my young daughter again. She was as sweet as ever and soon became the focus of my attention during my brief time away from the war.

When the week finally came to an end, we departed without so much as a goodbye. I was almost glad to return to Vietnam and my teammates. My wife had failed to offer any explanation for her sudden disinterest and, like a fool, I had failed to ask for one. My marriage appeared to be in deep trouble and I knew it, but there was nothing I could do about it at the time. I still had half my tour to complete and I knew that there wasn't anything that I could accomplish by mail that I had been unable to accomplish in person during my R&R. The rest of the story will be told later.

Chapter Seventeen

Just after Christmas, Lieutenant Hill told me to get my team ready for another mission. He would give us a briefing outside the barracks in ten minutes. I passed the word to my team and told them to gear up and join me for the briefing. O'Day was my ATL, Laure my senior RTO, Dien my point man, John Dilo was my junior RTO and Bellwood my rear security man. Like most of our missions in the Delta, we'd be going out 'light' with only our weapons and web gear.

We hurriedly put on our cammies and painted our faces with the standard Army issue camo sticks, then moved out to meet Lieutenant Hill for the pre-mission briefing. The Lieutenant told us that our mission was to locate an enemy POW camp suspected to be in the area. He gave us new maps covering an area we had never worked before, then provided the general coordinates for where S-2 thought the camp was located. It showed that the suspected POW compound was thought to be somewhere on a long spit of land located between a river and a secondary canal that emptied into it.

When the briefing ended, we moved to the helipad and boarded the waiting Huey. I showed the pilot the coordinates to where we wanted to insert. He nodded that he understood. We took up our usual positions on either side of the open cargo bay as the chopper went light on its skids, lifted off the PSP helipad, then nosed forward to pick up transitional airspeed. I looked at my teammates and gave them my usual 'thumbs up'. Every one of us was excited about the possibility of freeing friendly prisoners, especially if there were any Americans among them.

As the Huey approached our insertion point, it went into a quick hover 5ft above the LZ giving us the opportunity to step out on the skids and drop to the ground. As the helicopter lifted out and faded away in the distance, we took stock of our location and current situation. The chopper had put us in on a slightly elevated rise with the river on our right and a 15-meter-wide canal on our left. Some 300 meters to our front, the peninsula narrowed where the canal met the river. Surprisingly, there was little vegetation on the peninsula, or any signs of human activity. Either the Intel about the POW encampment on the peninsula was faulty or it had to be located underground.

I whispered to my teammates to be on the lookout for tunnel openings, then nodded for Dien to move out. We walked cautiously in patrol formation toward the point where the canal intersected the river, all the time searching for a possible underground entrance. I was a little nervous. There was little cover or concealment around us. I felt like we were overly exposed with nowhere to go if we ran into trouble.

When we had covered nearly half the distance to the end of the peninsula, I decided to walk over to the edge of the canal to see if there might be a tunnel entrance along the steep embankment. Weapon at the ready, I peered cautiously over the edge and began to scan the bank at the water-line 10ft below me.

Suddenly, movement up ahead caught my attention. I looked out towards the end of the canal and spotted two sampans, each manned by seven VC, coming down the river and preparing to turn into the canal. They were headed in our direction but were still 150 meters away. I signaled for the team to take cover back away from the canal behind a 2ft-high earthen berm that ran along the crest of the peninsula. I formulated a hasty plan to wait until the two sampans were out in the canal directly in front of our position, then on my signal we would leap to our feet, rush to the edge of the canal and open fire on them. We were outnumbered two to one, but we had the element of surprise on our side and the enemy soldiers were tightly massed in two small sampans. Unless we screwed up, it would be a massacre.

We waited breathlessly as the sampans moved closer and closer to where we lay hidden. The suspense was palpable. I looked at each of my fellow LRPs to make sure they were ready. It was almost time.

When I gave the signal to prepare to close on the canal, Dilo looked up at me and shook his head 'no' and refused to move. I could see the terror in his eyes. He could see the anger in mine. There was no time to convince him to change his mind, so I motioned for the rest of the team stay down and hold their positions. I didn't want Dilo behind us if we blew the ambush without him. If he 'lost it' and opened fire, I didn't want him shooting one or more of us in the back. I was mad as hell that one of my teammates had let me down, and for a couple of minutes I forgot about the VC in the sampans out in the canal. It was at that moment that a single VC suddenly appeared at the top of the canal bank directly in front of me. He appeared as surprised to see me as I was to see him. He hesitated, trying to decide what to do next. I didn't give him time to make the decision. I shot him in the chest and watched as he fell back into the canal. While we had been focused on Dilo, the damned VC had pulled into the shore right in front of us and were at that moment preparing to leave their boats.

We immediately began tossing our frags and concussion grenades over the embankment and into the water below us. After the explosions subsided, we leaped to our feet and began firing on full auto into the splintered sampans and the bodies at the edge of the canal. I was relieved when there was no return fire coming from the enemy soldiers.

It was dusk by then and growing darker by the minute. We had nowhere to go to avoid any VC who might have survived our onslaught. If they or any others in the vicinity came looking for us, we would be trapped on this narrow spit of land. The ground behind us was open and almost devoid of cover. We had water on both sides of us and a long way to go to find a place to hide for the remainder of the night. I knew that our brief firefight would not have gone unnoticed by any other VC in the area.

I made the decision to call for gunship support and an extraction aircraft. We pulled back in the direction of our original LZ and set up security until we heard the two Cobra gunships approaching from upriver. I got on the radio and gave them the coordinates where the sampans had attempted to land, then sat back and watched as the two aircraft made a couple of passes over the area, firing their mini-guns into the dead and wounded VC. While this was going on up the canal, the Huey extraction ship slipped in and hovered a few meters away from our position.

When the aircraft touched down, we leaped aboard and signaled the pilot to get us out of there in a hurry. As the chopper rose up and out over the canal, the port-side door gunner fired a long burst into the wreckage of both sampans, finishing off the job we and the Cobras had done on the VC. Finally, the door gunner shouted to us that it looked like there had been no survivors.

On the trip back to Tan An, I was boiling mad. My anger was directed primarily at Dilo, but I was also upset about how the mission had gone down. I had pulled more than forty missions with the LRPs and nothing like this had ever happened to me before. I was not only angry, but I was heartbroken that we had not been able to locate the POW compound or to find out if it even existed.

We landed back at camp and I went to see the Lieutenant for the debriefing. I did not tell him what Dilo had done, but I did indicate that he would not be going out on patrol with us again. He looked at me and said: 'Well what should I do with him?' I shook my head, shrugged my shoulders and replied: 'Put him on radio relay duty, or driving the jeep, or hell, L-T, let him polish your boots. I don't care. Just keep him away from me.'

The Lieutenant accepted my demand and pulled Dilo off the team the next day. He was assigned medial tasks back at Dong Tam until his tour ended. None of my teammates spoke of Dilo's cowardice and his failure to perform. We had managed to destroy the enemy unit without him. He would have to live with his shame. We made the decision not to make it worse for him.

Chapter Eighteen

I was sitting on my bunk on the evening of 31 December, still fuming over not locating the POW compound on my last mission. Dilo had been pulled off my team and given a job in the rear until his tour ended late in January. I felt sorry for him, but I couldn't afford to have a man on my team that I couldn't trust. There was no room for doubt in combat. If you couldn't rely on the men around you, then you knew it would only be a matter of time before you suffered casualties. War was a game of percentages, but 100 percent was the only one that made you a winner.

I was feeling melancholy and a little morose, maybe because the next day would be New Year's Day 1969, and I would be celebrating it waiting out the heavy rain in my barracks. To pass the time, I grabbed a ballpoint pen and a writing tablet and composed the following poem:

> Five Rangers leap from a chopper's side to run for the high grass
> Where they might hide.
> With camouflage suits and painted faces, all five Rangers would
> Take their places.
> In a single line they moved for cover and prayed their
> positions would
> Not be discovered,
> But alas, they were spotted by innocent civilians who would
> run and tell
> 'Charlie' of the Rangers insertion.
> As the team leader gave the command with the snap of a
> finger and
> The wave of a hand, to move to the jungle and try to evade,
> The oncoming enemy will not be delayed.
> It was late afternoon when the Vietcong were seen searching and
> Probing, looking raw and mean.

Wearing straw hats and black PJs, carrying carbines and AKs.
At the side of the trail, the Rangers made ready to engage the VC,
They'd have to be steady.
Over the radio they whispered, 'Have the gunships fly fast,'
For the enemy were many, the Ranger may not last.
They could hear the voices chanting with a sing song sing.
Oh, how it did make their ears ring!
Forgive us, O Lord, for what we must do
To survive, O Lord, we believe in you.
With the sound of gunfire came flashes of light,
Meaning the contact had started and now they must fight.
The VC advanced with guns at the ready,
But the Rangers' fight was both hard and steady.
For every one downed,
Two more stood his ground.
Then the gunships came in with a whine,
And broke the Vietcong line.
The brave group of Rangers then retreated,
As the slick came in all five were seated.
The men stood strong and brave that day,
And they thanked the Lord, they knew how to pray.
Off to their base camp for a well-earned rest,
Then off once again for another brave test.

Chapter Nineteen

On 23 January 1969, my platoon leader, First Lieutenant Robert Hill, approached me and announced that I needed to get my team together for a mission. I rounded up Mike O'Day, Steve Lauer, Richard Bellwood and Willy Boone and proceeded to S-3 (Brigade Operations) for the pre-mission briefing. When we were all seated, Lieutenant Hill told us that S-2 had just received some reliable Intel that enemy troops had just been sighted moving in and out of an isolated building near a village a few klicks out from our Brigade base camp at Tan An. S-3 wanted a long-range patrol team to go in and find out what the VC were up to. Tango 1-1 had been given the mission.

Since the area consisted of large numbers of flooded rice paddies surrounding dozens of tiny hamlets, I decided to go out on an overflight to select a suitable LZ within eyeshot of the target building. I asked Lieutenant Hill to lay on an LOH scout helicopter for the flight out to my AO.

A short time later, I looked down on the hamlet where the building was said to be located and finally spotted it, sitting by itself within a few meters of a nearby rice paddy. I could see that it would be almost impossible to approach it without drawing attention from anyone in the area. I finally selected an open area about 100 meters away from the building for our LZ. It was the only open spot anywhere near our target, and we'd still have to cross a flooded rice paddy to get to it. I didn't like the set-up, but there was no suitable alternative.

When I got back to Tan An, I told my two PRUs (South Vietnamese soldiers serving with the local Provisional Reconnaissance Units) who were often part of my team to get their gear ready for the mission. There would be seven of us going out on the patrol. As usual, we would be going in 'light' with only our weapons, web gear and a pair of radios. We put on our camouflage fatigues and applied our 'war paint' to cover our exposed body parts.

I decided that I would carry my 'specialized' CAR-15 on the patrol. Back in December, right after my promotion, I noticed that the rate of fire of a CAR-15 was far too high. It was an ammo-burner that emptied a twenty-round magazine in a matter of seconds. Reloading in the middle of a firefight meant that the enemy had time to fire at you without having to duck your rounds. I decided to slow down the weapon's cyclic rate of fire, so I removed the stock assembly from my M16 and placed it on my CAR-15. It worked like a charm. The longer spring from the M16 slowed the rate of fire, yet the shorter barrel allowed me to still have a more compact weapon.

We arrived at the chopper pad where I gave the pilot the coordinates of the LZ I had selected and told him that I would indicate the exact spot where I wanted him to put us down when we reached the area. He nodded his approval. I folded my map and shoved it into the cargo pocket on the side of my tiger fatigue pants and signaled for my teammates to board the waiting Huey. As the familiar whine of the helicopter turbine began to grow louder, I squeezed in behind the pilot, gave my teammates a knowing grin followed by a wink and a 'thumbs-up', then sat back to enjoy the brief flight out to our recon zone.

When the chopper neared the coordinates I had selected, I pointed to a clearing 100 meters from the target hooch and motioned for the pilot to land there. The aircraft flared over the open area as my teammates and I stepped out on the skids and leaped into the waist-high cover on the landing zone. Lightened by our departure, the aircraft rose quickly into the sky and headed back toward Tan An.

We remained motionless, squatting in the sparse cover for a few moments, listening and monitoring the area around us. I knew that the target hooch was not far away, so I decided to divide the team into two elements and approach it from both sides, hoping to catch the occupants in a crossfire. I whispered to Mike O'Day, my ATL, to take Lauer, Bellwood and Boone to the left side of the structure, and I would take the two PRUs and move in from the right side.

We had to move through nearly 100 meters of underbrush and then cross a waist-deep irrigation ditch to reach the paddy dike just short of the building. My element had further to go to get to our position, so we were forced to move rapidly.

In the process of maneuvering to our designated jump-off points, the VC inside the building spotted O'Day's group. Realizing that we had lost the element of surprise, O'Day made the decision to initiate contact and opened fire on the enemy troops.

As a full-fledged firefight broke out, I heard the VC firing an RPD machine gun from inside the hooch. After a brief burst, it suddenly fell silent. I didn't know if it had jammed, the gunner had been hit or had decided to '*di di mau*' (flee) the area.

That's when I noticed seven Viet Cong breaking through the door of the hooch and sprinting straight toward me and my two PRUs. We were standing in the open in knee-deep water with the nearest cover, a paddy dike, still 50 meters away.

Without thinking, I took off, sloshing through the water straight at the enemy soldiers. I was firing my weapon as I ran, frustrated at the water slowing down my forward momentum. I remember thinking: 'Shit, there are seven of them and only one of me.' It suddenly hit me that these were the same odds that Custer had faced at the Little Bighorn. I knew instinctively that I had to put as many rounds down-range as I could to prevent the VC from focusing on the crazy American soldier splashing awkwardly towards them. Thankfully, my two PRUs were hot on my tail, but their proximity to my wide backside prevented them from joining in the battle. I was on my own.

One of my rounds caught the lead VC in the torso. I saw his weapon disappear into the paddy water as he went down with a splash behind it. Then I hit a second one and saw him go down next to the first one, only to pop right back up again and continue running toward me.

When the six remaining VC had closed to within 30 meters of me and my PRUs, they suddenly turned left and sprinted down the paddy dike and disappeared behind a cluster of nearby huts.

I stopped my insane rush and stood there, dripping sweat and muddy water into the rice paddy, gasping and trying to catch my breath. My two PRUs came up to me and pointed to the spot where the surviving VC had just disappeared. I shook my head, indicating that I had no intention of chasing after them. My momma had not raised any dummies.

When we linked up with the rest of the team, I noticed that Bellwood was holding a compress dressing to his neck. I walked over to him to see what was wrong and discovered that he had taken a piece of shrapnel in the side of his neck. I could see that the wound was not life-threatening, but would need to be treated as soon as we got back to the base camp. I grinned at Bellwood and said: 'Well, Richie, I guess you'll be wanting a Purple Heart for that, huh?' He shrugged his shoulders, then nodded, garnering laughter from the rest of the team.

O'Day stepped into the hooch to check it for anything the VC may have left behind and was surprised to discover two South Vietnamese police officers and their wives lying bound and gagged on the floor. They were being held captive by the VC we had just chased off. We quickly released them and pulled the tape off their mouths. They were overjoyed at being rescued. Naturally, they attributed their salvation to us and made it generally known how grateful they were for our intervention. We were equally elated to have been able to release them from their captivity. The only thing that could have made it any better for us would have been if there were Americans there, too. The rescue was indeed a bonus for my teammates and I, since there had been no mention of possible captives during the pre-mission briefing.

I told my RTO, Lauer, to call Command and tell them we would need a pair of slicks for the extraction: one for the freed captives and one for our team. We then moved them to a more secure location out in the open and waited for the two choppers to arrive.

Ten minutes later, we heard the Hueys off in the distance. I popped a smoke grenade to mark our position and watched as the first aircraft moved in and touched down a few meters away, followed by the second chopper landing 30 meters behind it. We helped the four Vietnamese aboard the first Huey, then climbed aboard the second ship for the quick trip back to our base camp.

Division Headquarters must have thought that it was a better-than-average mission, because everyone on the team was soon awarded Bronze Stars with 'V' device for the operation. The South Vietnamese government also showed its appreciation for saving four of its citizens by awarding each of us the Vietnamese Cross of Gallantry. It was all in a day's work in the LRPs.

Chapter Twenty

On the morning after the January 23rd mission, I was sitting on my footlocker in the barracks cleaning my weapon when Lieutenant Hill walked in and said: 'Sergeant Thayer, I was wondering if you could do me a favor.' I stopped what I was doing and answered: 'Well, Sir, if it's within my ability to do so I'd be happy to.' He smiled and continued: 'I've got a friend who's a major with the 6th of the 31st Infantry and he asked me if I knew of anyone who could interrogate a VC prisoner they captured. S-2 had no luck getting anything out of him and I thought that maybe you and one of your PRUs might give it a try.' I considered it for a moment, then said: 'Well, Lieutenant, let me grab one of my boys and we'll give it a go.' He thanked me and left to go back to the orderly room to contact the major and tell him we'd be there in a short time.

I found Bao and told him what I needed. He got this huge grin on his face and told me that he would be happy to go with me.

When we arrived at the infantry compound on the other side of the Tan An base camp, we met the major who said that the prisoner was under guard in the back of the S-2 building. He showed us to where the VC sat under guard, hand-cuffed to a chair. I told the major that we'd like to be alone with him. The officer nodded, then he and the guard stepped out of the room and closed the door behind them.

For the next fifteen minutes, Bao interrogated the stoic VC. I don't have any idea what he told the man or if he threatened him and his heirs in any way, but by the end of the discussion the prisoner suddenly started talking and would not shut up. During the course of his interrogation, he told Bao of the location of a regimental-sized enemy unit hidden in a large patch of forest 12 klicks outside Tan An. When Bao had finished speaking to the now broken man, he related to me what the VC had told him. I thanked Bao for his success, then went out and repeated the information to the major who seemed somewhat doubtful of the veracity of the report. I told him that he could believe it or not, that was his choice. He told us that he appreciated our effort and would send it up the chain of command, then Bao and I left to return to our barracks.

Chapter Twenty-One

The next day, 25 January, Tango 1-1 got an op order for another mission. It was a little after 1000 hours in the morning when Lieutenant Hill found me and said:

> Sergeant Thayer, S-3 has decided to check out the information you got out of the VC prisoner yesterday. They want to send a team in to recon that patch of woods the prisoner spoke about. I've got a chopper waiting on the helipad right now for you to go on an overflight to check out the area. I would recommend that you select an LZ outside the area, away from the forest, so that you can get in without being observed.

He handed me a map with the coordinates the VC had indicated written on the acetone cover in grease pencil. 'Roger that, Lieutenant, I'm on it,' I responded, accepting the map.

I grabbed my weapon and a bandolier of loaded magazines and ran down to the helipad. An LOH was sitting there waiting for me. I climbed into the tiny scout helicopter and showed the pilot the location I wanted to check out. After putting on a flight helmet and making sure the intercom mic was working, I nodded to the pilot that I was ready to go. Our target area was 12 klicks (7 miles) west of Tan An, out in the Plain of Reeds, just north of the village of Phu My in Dinh Truong Province.

The Plain of Reeds was a vast marshland covered in aquatic reeds and was unsuitable for farming. There were few villages in the area. There were occasional rice paddies where villagers from outside the area had managed to clear away the prolific reeds in a valiant attempt to make the land productive. There were also numerous tree-lines and long patches of woods where drier ground gave other flora a chance to take root and grow to maturity.

We flew over the area at high altitude to avoid alerting anyone on the ground. I could make out a canal running through the center of a rather large, dense wooded area that stretched about 500 to 600 meters in length and was nearly 100 meters wide. I noticed that there were several patches of trees jutting out from the main wooded area into the reeds and kunai grass. Some of them were a good 100 meters long and 50 meters wide. The entire area was easily large enough to hide an NVA regiment. I noticed that the wood-line tapered down to only a few meters wide at the south-eastern end. There was not enough cover there to hide anyone, so I selected a landing zone 100 meters west of that point in an open area where the grass appeared shorter than normal. I marked the location on my map, then signaled the pilot that I was ready to go back to Tan An.

Back on the helipad I thanked the pilot and headed back to the barracks to round up my team. We grabbed our gear and went to the Operations shed to go over our plans with Lieutenant Hill. When we were done, Lieutenant Hill wished us good luck and we moved out for the helipad.

The single Huey was waiting for us when we got there, and we wasted little time climbing aboard. I wanted to get this patrol over with and get back to Tan An before dark. We lifted off, swinging around to the west. I was wearing a brand-new pair of tiger fatigues and my usual camo headband. I decided at the last minute to leave behind my CAR-15 in favor of a heavier but longer-shooting M14. We would be operating in a vast open area where the ability to 'reach out and touch someone' was more than a likely possibility.

I cast a glance at each team member and gave them my usual 'thumbs up' to assure them that everything was going as planned. My American teammates were wearing the standard-issue camo fatigues and boonie hats. My two PRUs, Bao and Dien, were wearing tiger-stripe camos, just like the fatigues I was wearing. From previous missions, I had developed a great confidence in these local indigenous soldiers. They had proven to be loyal, brave and possessed great combat skills. The PRUs were small units of tough, tested Vietnamese paramilitary personnel. They were highly-skilled combat veterans who had survived years of combat in regular South Vietnamese military units before coming to the PRU. All of them claimed a deep hatred for the VC due to the atrocities committed against them and their families by the guerrilla forces. It was not unusual for our teams to take out one or two PRUs on given missions. They were a solid part of our teams and were invaluable for their knowledge of the enemy and their ability to interpret for us when the need arose.

When we neared our recon zone, the Huey dropped from altitude down to approximately 30ft above ground level to approach our LZ. Seated in the open cargo doors with our legs dangling above the skids, we waited for the Huey to slow to a hover above our insertion point.

As the aircraft came to a stop a few feet above the ground, we took turns sliding out on the skids and dropping off into the high grass beneath us. When the last man was safely away from the chopper, it lifted out and returned to base.

We sprinted to a position behind a long earthen berm, not far from our LZ. It was 3 to 4ft high and offered both cover and concealment while we took stock of our position. I knew immediately without checking my map that the pilot had dropped us in the wrong location. We were 100 meters from the spot I had selected and were on the south-east side of where we wanted to be and not the North side where I wanted to be.

I had no choice now that we were committed. We would have to make the best of the hand we'd been dealt. I checked our map and determined that we were approximately 50 meters south-west of a wooded area bordering the Rach Lang Cat Canal. The grass to our front was only knee-high, offering no cover or concealment between the berm and the woods. Our only course of action was to cross this open area to reach the wood-line without being observed.

On my signal, the team assembled into patrol formation and moved out over the berm toward the nearby tree-line. Bao had taken the point position, while Dien moved back to the rear of the file to secure the drag or trail position.

As we neared the trees, Bao threw up his left hand to stop the team. He had sensed something and turned to the left, walking parallel to the tree-line, cautiously inspecting the woods before entering them. Suddenly, an NVA soldier, dressed in a khaki uniform, wearing olive drab web gear, stood up out of the cover and leveled his AK-47 at my point man. I was directly behind Bao in the 'slack' position and saw what was about to happen. I raised the M14 to my shoulder and dropped the NVA 10ft away before he had a chance to squeeze the trigger.

At that moment, a heavy barrage of gunfire erupted from the woods as a full platoon of NVA soldiers opened up on us from less than 15 meters away. Some of my teammates immediately dropped to a knee to return fire, while others began moving to their left or right to prevent the enemy soldiers from drawing a bead on them. We had been caught out in the open in front of the woods with the nearest cover a distant 50 meters behind us. We were heavily outnumbered and engaged in a battle that was now raging all along the tree-line.

Out of my peripheral vision, I saw Mike O'Day to my left chasing down an NVA soldier wearing a pith helmet and scrambling along the edge of the woods. O'Day stopped, shouldered his rifle and put a single round through the back of the soldier's neck, tumbling him into the heavy vegetation.

Further to my left, I spotted Bao and Dien standing side by side in the open engaged in a heated exchange with the NVA soldiers hidden back in the trees. They were alternately firing their rifles, then shouting back and forth in Vietnamese. Interspersed among the rapid-fire lingo, I could make out an occasional 'F**k you!' I would later learn that the NVA were trying to convince the PRUs to turn on their American counterparts and kill them, promising to spare their lives if they did so. Their attempt served only to increase the resolve of the PRUs to fight to the death.

My RTO, Bellwood, was kneeling to my left rear calling in the contact on the radio. When he finished he yelled at me: 'What do you want me to do?' I shouted back at him: 'Shoot!' Bellwood dropped the radio handset and began firing his M16 at the NVA in the woods. Seconds later, he took a round in the right hip and went down, screaming at me that he'd been hit. I turned to see him struggling to get back up and ran to his side. I dropped to one knee and cradled his neck in the crook of my arm. At that moment, a single NVA stood up a few feet away and opened up on us with his AK-47 on full auto. Two rounds struck Bellwood in the chest, knocking him unconscious. One round hit me hard in the right shoulder, while other rounds hit my canteen, an ammo pouch and shot out the crystals on both my wrist compass and my watch. (Many years later I would give the compass and watch bands to Bellwood's nephew.)

I dropped to the ground and rolled to the right away from my unconscious RTO. I came up firing from the hip and dropped the NVA soldier who had just shot me and Bellwood. The enemy staggered backwards and collapsed into the underbrush behind him. I realized that for us to survive the battle I would have to get some air support on the scene in the next few minutes. I spotted the radio lying next to Bellwood, but I could see that it had taken a couple of rounds and was not operational.

I crawled to the right along the edge of the tree-line, searching for the other RTO. Over the sounds of the firefight, I shouted: 'LAUER... LAUER!' 'HERE,' he replied. I crawled over to the sound of his voice and found him wounded but still on his feet, moving and firing into the trees.

Something inexplicable occurred at that moment. I felt a strange presence near me. I thought it was my imagination playing tricks on me, but then a memory from my childhood flooded into my thoughts. My great-grandmother was a full-blooded Cherokee named Dreaming Woman. Her daughter, my grandmother, was Sara Dreamer and my aunt's name was Alice Dreamer. My grandmother had died when I was 6 years old so I barely remembered her, but my aunt used to tell me stories of the old days and instructed me to always pay attention to my dreams and my visions.

While crawling toward Lauer, the pace of the battle seemed to slow down. I felt an unmistakable presence of someone or something that was with me. At first, I thought it was my older brother Ray, who had been killed in the Second World War. Then I was not sure. It could have been my guardian angel or a spirit or maybe God himself. Maybe it was just luck. I didn't know, and don't know to this day. All I can say for certain is that something protected me that day. My aunt had told me that I would be watched over by those who had passed before me. It was spooky.

When I reached Lauer he told me that he had already reported our contact. I took the handset from his radio and called for artillery and gunship support, then called our radio relay team at an outpost near Phu My village, telling them: 'We've got gooks everywhere. They're all over the damn place. At least a platoon or a full company of NVA regulars.' The relay team told me to hold on, that gunship support was on the way to our location. The relay team then contacted 3rd Brigade Headquarters and reported that we were engaged with at least an NVA company. Seconds later, two Cobra gunships from D Troop, 3rd of the 5th Air Cavalry arrived over our embattled LRP team. The Cobras were able to see the team scattered out in the open terrain 10 to 15 meters in front of the woods. It was obvious to both pilots that the LRPs were in a fight for their lives.

The pilot of the lead aircraft came up on our radio frequency and asked: 'Tango 1-1, this is Crusader 3-6 with a pair of gunships. How can we help?' I answered back: 'Hit everything in the woods to our front.' The pilot replied: 'You got it.'

The lead Cobra banked to the left in a descending turn out over the open area behind us. Leveling off at 50ft above the ground, he flew directly toward our position. Coming to an abrupt hover above and just behind us, the chopper hung boldly in the air like a mother hen guarding her chicks, except this mother hen was heavily armed. Commencing pedal turns to cover the entire tree-line, the gunship began blasting the wood-line, first with blazing mini-guns, then aerial rockets and finally 40mm grenades. Amazingly, the NVA stood their ground and fired back at the hovering Cobra. While we watched the courageous aircrew tearing the woods apart, his wingman made a wide circle to our left and took up a position about 200ft above the end of the tree-line and began expending his ordnance into the smoking vegetation.

With the wound in my shoulder, I could only fire my weapon from my hip. I managed to empty two more magazines into the NVA positions before I heard the familiar 'wop, wop, wop, wop' of an approaching Huey. There was no other sound like it in the world.

The helicopter approached low from the south and flared to a landing not more than 30 meters behind our position, its right-side open cargo door facing the now shattered woods. When the Huey touched down, the first Cobra executed a pedal turn to the left and lifted off to the west to join his wingman still on station firing up the tree-line. The two gunships took turns covering us as we began to withdraw to the waiting slick.

O'Day and Boone grabbed Bellwood under each arm and dragged him to the waiting helicopter as the door gunner kept the NVA at bay with his M60 machine gun. As soon as they had Bellwood aboard, I shouted for the rest of the team to 'MOUNT UP!'

The remaining three team members broke contact and sprinted for the chopper. I was right behind them, trying to pop off a couple more rounds into the tree-line. O'Day and Boone helped to pull me on board as the helicopter went light on its skids and lifted off to the south-west. Realizing we had wounded aboard, the courageous pilot headed directly to the aid station at Tan An.

On the brief trip back to our base camp I realized that more than half my team had been wounded in the battle back at the tree-line. Richie Bellwood's wounds were life-threatening. I said a silent prayer that he would make it. I shoved my way to the gap between the pilot and co-pilot and shouted for them to hurry.

When the Huey touched down on the medical pad at Tan An, a half-dozen medics rushed out to the aircraft and lifted Bellwood onto a gurney, then wheeled him into triage. The rest of us followed closely behind. Inside, Bellwood was placed on an operating table where the med team started working on him. I could see that he was in good hands. Another medic told me to hop up on the table so he could check out my wound. After cutting off my shirt, he told me that there was no exit wound, which meant that the bullet was lodged somewhere in my back. They would have to medevac me to the hospital at Tan Son Nhut in Saigon to have the bullet surgically removed.

While the medic was wrapping my shoulder, I looked over at Bellwood and saw that there was no longer anyone working on him. I knew immediately that he had died. With tears welling up in my eyes, I continued to stare at my friend and teammate lying unattended on the bloody gurney. One of the doctors who was standing nearby looked at me and said: 'What's wrong with you, soldier, you're not hit that bad?' I looked up at him through the tears. 'You think I'm worried about this?' I snarled, pointing at my shoulder. 'This ain't shit. That's my friend lying over there.' My blood pressure reached boiling-point and I leaped off the table. Bao was standing close to me and still had his weapon. I grabbed it, but he held on, unwilling to let me take it from him. Lieutenant Hill, who had just walked into the triage area, saw what was happening and shouted: 'SERGEANT THAYER, DON'T SHOOT HIM.' The doctor, sensing that he was better off leaving the area, moved out rapidly without looking back.

The medic who had been attending me checked Richie, then put his hand on my good shoulder and said: 'He's gone. There's nothing else we can do.' I was absolutely devastated. Richie Bellwood had been like a kid brother to me. I couldn't control my grief.

A short time later, I was loaded aboard a Huey Dust-Off and medevacked to Saigon for surgery on my shoulder. During the flight, I kept seeing Richie's lifeless body on the gurney in the triage room. There was another wounded soldier on the stretcher in the rack above me; I could only see his blond hair and kept imagining it was Bellwood. I reached up and grabbed his hand and talked to him all the way to Saigon. When we arrived at Tan Son Nhut and they unloaded us onto gurneys, I saw the other soldier's face and realized it was not Bellwood. I thought to myself that I must be losing my mind. I needed to get a grip on myself.

They wheeled us into an operating room where a surgeon told me that he would be removing the bullet from my shoulder. A medic began to cut my pants off from down by my ankle. I told the doctor to please not cut off my belt. He smiled and pulled off the belt with my K-Bar attached, wrapped the belt around the sheath and slipped it under my gurney. He said: 'Don't worry, Sergeant, it will go wherever you go.' I thanked him as the anesthetist moved to the head of the table to see that I would sleep through the surgery.

When I awoke several hours later, a medic told me that Major General Julian Ewell, the Commanding Officer of the 9th Infantry Division, was on his way to the hospital to see me. A short time later, the general, accompanied by Captain Dickey, came walking down the aisle in the open ward and stopped at the side of my bed. I remember the general saying with a smile as I tried to get to my feet: 'You just sit on the bed, soldier.' In a brief ceremony, General Ewell presented me with the Silver Star and a Purple Heart. He then told me that he was promoting me to staff sergeant. I was totally surprised. I was even more surprised when Lieutenant Hill showed up for the ceremony. He had broken protocol to hitch a ride to Saigon. I thought how cool it was for him to do that.

After the general and Captain Dickey had left, Lieutenant Hill informed me that Richard Bellwood had been posthumously awarded the Silver Star and Purple Heart. O'Day and Lauer had also received the same awards and had been promoted to sergeant. Boone had been awarded the Bronze Star with 'V' device.

Lieutenant Hill told me that I didn't realize what our team had accomplished. He said that we had taken out more than thirty NVA soldiers during the battle. Subsequent gunship strikes, artillery fire missions and finally a sweep by an infantry company took out another 120 or more.

We discovered a few days later that it was very likely that our team had intercepted an NVA battalion on its way to attack the 3rd Brigade compound at Tan An during the numerous attacks that occurred all across Vietnam commencing on the night of 31 January 1968, the beginning of the Tet holiday.

Chapter Twenty-Two

Not long after the general and my commanding officer had departed and Lieutenant Hill had returned to Tan An, a medic showed up and gave me a shot of something that knocked me out. I recall waking up on a plane for a minute or two, not sure of where I was, then going right back to sleep again. The next thing I remember was hearing a distant voice saying: 'Can you hear me, son?'

I fought my way through the thick haze that had engulfed me, finally snapping out of it to find a doctor standing there next to me. I was lying in a clean bed on nice, crisp sheets in a brightly-lit room. The doctor told me that I was at Camp Zama Hospital in Japan. He said that they were going to unwrap my shoulder to check my wound and clean it before putting on a fresh dressing. I nodded, still unsure what was going on.

Using a long swab, the doctor probed the hole in my shoulder, then dipped the swabs in hydrogen peroxide and dabbed them deep into the wound. It hurt like hell, but I didn't let him know it. The doctor announced that they would have to clean my wound two or three times a day for the next five days to avoid an infection. I didn't say anything, but nodded that I understood. It was not something I would be looking forward to.

A medic came in and handed me a phone, saying: 'We had placed a call to your wife back in the States, Sergeant. She's on the line now.' I took the phone and said 'Hello.' I heard her respond with 'Hello.' I told her that I had been wounded but not too bad, and that they were taking good care of me. She responded: 'Okay.' There was no warmth or concern in her voice. I told her that I had no shaving gear, toothbrush or anything and asked her to wire me a few dollars so I could buy what I needed. I had been sending almost my entire paycheck home for the past six months, so I knew that she could afford to send me a small amount of money.

I was shocked when I heard her say 'NO!' I suddenly remembered the way I had felt when I met her in Hawaii for my R&R. It was not something I had imagined. It was true, my marriage was over. She had just confirmed it for me.

I was dealing with a lot at that moment, and the last thing I wanted was to get into a long-distance argument with her. Plus I was ashamed to say anything in front of the doctor and the medic standing next to my bed. Before I could say anything else, she hung up the phone on me. I said to the dial tone: 'Well okay, don't worry about me. I'll call you back later. Goodbye.' I hung up, handed the phone back to the medic and thanked him.

The doctor told me that he was going to give me a couple of shots: one an antibiotic and the other one for pain. I rolled over on my left side so he could inject me in the buttocks.

I woke up sometime later in a long ward with a lot of other wounded servicemen. There were approximately fifty beds on the ward and each one was occupied. There was a wounded lieutenant in the bed next to me. He was a very nice guy and we talked a lot over the next few days. He had been shot several times by a Chicom RPD machine gun. His wounds were serious. When the doctor came to clean them and change his bandages, the pain was dreadful for him to endure. The poor guy suffered a lot. After seeing what he had to go through, I managed to quietly accept the discomfort when my own wound was cleaned. I was ashamed to cry out or flinch, thinking about what he had to go through.

The first day I was there, someone from the Red Cross came to the ward and gave me some shaving gear, a toothbrush, toothpaste and a few other things. So it turned out that I wouldn't be needing any money after all.

It wasn't long before my emotional wellbeing began to suffer. I was laid up in a hospital in a foreign country, dealing with a painful wound, reliving the mission that had put me there, grieving over the loss of Bellwood, and wondering what had happened to the rest of my teammates. All day and all night, I had to listen to other wounded soldiers screaming and crying out in pain or experiencing horrid nightmares. In addition, I had lost my baby girl and was unable to do anything about it because of where I was halfway round the world.

On the morning of my third day at Camp Zama, I was lying on my left side while a medic was poking a swab 3in into my shoulder wound and another one in the surgical wound in my back. I buried my face in the pillow to keep from screaming and to absorb the tears pouring from my eyes. It was a combination of the physical pain and the emotional strain I was going through that was causing my stress. I tried my best to hold it inside me where no one could see it. I felt totally alone, totally abandoned, totally helpless. My teammates were scattered and I didn't know where they were or what had happened to them. My wife had tossed me to the wolves without an explanation. I didn't care so much about losing her – our love had died a long time ago – but I couldn't forgive her for the way she did it. I felt like I was drifting in space, untethered and uncontrolled. I had no purpose in life anymore. Lying around in a hospital waiting for my wound to heal was not part of my DNA. That's when I decided that I needed to have a talk with the major in charge of the recovery wing of the hospital the very next day.

The next morning, I made my way to the major's office. I thanked him for seeing me and explained my situation to him. I told him that I really needed to get off the ward. I went through the entire litany of reasons why I just had to get out of there. After listening attentively to my predicament, he totally surprised me when he said: 'I think I can help you, Sergeant. First, we'll get you a new ID card. As an E-6, you don't need a pass to leave the post. Second, we'll close the wound in your shoulder this afternoon so that you can transfer to the recovery barracks. Third, I'll make sure you get an advance in pay until your payroll records catch up to you.' He smiled, then laughed and said: 'By the way, Sergeant, I have your knife and belt in my safe. I'll give them back to you if you decide to return to Vietnam in the future.'

I had totally forgotten about the knife and belt that the doctor back in Saigon had placed under my gurney before my surgery. The officer had been true to his word. He had my deepest respect.

Chapter Twenty-Three

The major also proved to be a man of his word. By that evening I was in possession of a new ID card, my wound had been sutured shut and I had $200 in my pocket. Dressed only in hospital pajamas and a robe, I hurried off to the post exchange to buy what I needed to make my escape to freedom.

When I entered the PX, a civilian working there asked if he could help me with anything. I nodded and said: 'Yes. I need some pants and a loose shirt or sweater that won't tear the wire stitches out of my shoulder.' He looked at me like I was nuts, until I pulled the robe off my shoulder and showed him the wire sticking about an inch through my pajamas. He gulped and muttered: 'I think this kind of sweater might work for you.' He pulled a thick, bulky-knit sweater from a hanger and held it up for me to approve. When I nodded, he helped me out of my robe and pajama top, then held the sweater while I gingerly eased my arm into the sleeve. Sure enough, the wire poked through the loose weave of the sweater without pulling or snagging. When I finally got to looking halfway presentable, he helped me back into my sling. Ten minutes later, I was wearing a comfortable pair of denim jeans, along with a new pair of white crew socks and my Army-issue low quarters. I was all set and ready to go.

Thanking the clerk for his assistance, I left the PX and headed for the main gate. I flashed my new ID card to the two MPs stationed there. They looked at it approvingly and indicated that I could pass through. I shot them a knowing grin, and left the hospital compound behind me in search of the nearest bar where I could kick back and relax. At that point in time, my only desire was to drown my problems in copious draughts of beer.

I avoided the nearby bars where I spotted other soldiers hanging out. I wasn't looking for company, especially the company of other GIs.

I'd had enough of that on the hospital ward. I walked for perhaps a mile before I discovered a Japanese bar with no Americans inside. When I entered and took a seat at the bar, my thoughts went immediately to my failed marriage and the loss of my baby girl. Most of my sorrow was from the thought of losing her. I'd sensed the marriage was over when I met my wife on my R&R. She had been cold and remote and totally devoid of any interest in me or the dangers I was facing in Vietnam. The brief call to her when I arrived at Camp Zama confirmed my suspicions. I knew she had found someone else, and for the first time I realized that I really didn't care.

The bar was small, accommodating perhaps twenty-five to thirty customers. It was only half full at the time I arrived. The staff consisted of a sullen bartender and a few girls waiting tables. A few minutes after I took a seat at a table in the back of the bar, some of the girls came over to see my arm sling and the wire protruding through my sweater. Fortunately, they all spoke a little English and for the first time in a long time I felt myself actually enjoying the conversation. They wanted to know what happened to me, but not wanting to explain the details, I just told them that it was the war in Vietnam.

Their concern and willingness to spend time with me soon had me feeling pretty good about my decision to find a GI-free bar. The girls were exceptionally friendly and sweet as could be. They were also very pleasant to look at. One of the girls asked me if I was 'honglee'. God, I had been so excited to get away from the hospital that I had forgotten to eat dinner. I told her that I was indeed 'honglee' and ordered a bowl of noodles.

When the noodles arrived, the bartender brought me an Asahi beer. While the rest of the girls drifted away to take care of their other customers, the young lady who had asked me if I was hungry stayed by my side and began carrying on a more detailed conversation. We talked and laughed for over an hour. I had totally forgotten about all my troubles. Suddenly, she told the bartender that she was leaving with me, took my good hand and led me out of the bar.

I soon found out that her name was Mitsuko. We spent the next five days together visiting the beautiful sites in and around the area. The Japanese were famous for their beautiful flower gardens, Shinto shrines, pagodas and impressive buildings. We traveled by train, bus, taxi and rickshaw and had a wonderful time.

After the first day, I found myself confused. She had not asked for money or favors or anything else. We had rented a nice room at a hotel in Yokohama the first night. She had asked me if I was okay and if I was in pain. I told her that I had a bottle of pain pills my doctor had given me if the pain got too bad. She said something in Japanese that I didn't understand, then put her hand on my forehead and whispered: 'Good night, Jimmy Son.'

The only thing I remember about that first night was rolling on my opposite side so I wouldn't lie on my stitches. I slept like a baby for the first time in a long while. I was thankful I had found her. When I was with her, the devils that haunted me remained at bay. Mitsuko helped me deal with my emotions and made me forget the recent tragedies in my life.

The next day, she took me to a mall that had a lot of stores. I bought more pants, another sweater and a few other things I needed to fill my wardrobe. We even rented a car for the day and went for a drive. It didn't take me long to get pulled over for driving in the wrong lane. Fearing I would be arrested, I was pleasantly surprised when the policeman merely pointed out the lane I was supposed to be driving in. Mitsuko thought it was hilarious.

The five days passed too fast. We parted company with me promising to come and see her again. Unfortunately, it was not to happen. When I checked back in to the recovery ward at Camp Zama, they kept me there for two weeks before they finally removed the stitches in my shoulder. Immediately afterwards, I was assigned to a rehab ward to begin a program of intense physical therapy. I started working out with light weights and doing mild stretching exercises. As I grew stronger and the scar tissue began to loosen, additional weights were added to my routine and the stretching exercises became more frequent and more radical.

Finally, I was able to tell my doctor that I was just about back to normal and I wanted to rejoin my unit in Vietnam. He told me he wanted to see how well I could use my arm before he would release me back to duty. He ordered me to perform a series of physical tests. I did the best I could to show him that I could do anything he asked. Thank God, the doctor never had me straighten my arm overhead. It was the one thing that I still couldn't accomplish. I did, however, do everything else that he required me to do, including aiming a weapon, pretending to fire it and then reload.

It was another two weeks before the hospital finally cut orders for me to return to my unit in Dong Tam. True to his word, the major showed up as I was clearing the post and handed me my K-Bar knife, sheath and belt for my return to Vietnam. I was ready to go back to the war.

Chapter Twenty-Four

While I had been languishing in the hospital in Japan, the Department of the Army had reorganized all thirteen long-range patrol companies in Vietnam into lettered Ranger companies under the 75th Infantry as part of the combat arms regimental system. My unit, Company E, 50th Infantry (LRP) had been deactivated, then immediately reactivated as Company E, 75th Infantry (Ranger). We were now known as 'Echo Rangers' or 'Riverine Rangers' because our area of operations was in the watery Mekong Delta area of South Vietnam.

Nothing had really changed for us. We still had the same personnel, pulling the same kind of missions, in the same general area of IV Corps. Only our title was different. It would take us a while to get used to being called 'Rangers' instead of 'LRPs'. We would never know if the enemy ever noticed the difference. We sure didn't. However, being Rangers ensured that we had been given a proud heritage to live up to. Rangers in the US Army went all the way back to the Revolutionary War. Their counterparts had fought on both sides in the Civil War, Second World War and Korea. We would have some rather big shoes to fill, but we felt confident that we could do the job and make our forefathers proud.

Chapter Twenty-Five

My plane touched down at Tan Son Nhut Air Base, Republic of South Vietnam on 15 March 1969. I grabbed my bag, walked off the base and hailed a pedicab. I told the driver to take me to the nearest bar. Sometime during my flight back to Vietnam, I realized that I was depressed again and couldn't understand why. I had wanted to come back to Nam and to my unit. With my marriage shot, nothing else seemed to matter to me. Now that I was back in-country, I wasn't sure anymore if this was what I really wanted. I didn't know it at the time, but the symptoms of PTSD were already manifesting themselves in my psyche.

I'd almost forgotten how hot Vietnam was during my six-week sojourn in the mild winter weather of Japan. I was soaked with sweat by the time the driver pulled up to a local bar a mile from the air base. I paid him and hurriedly stepped inside. Three ceiling fans moved the stagnant air around the bar, making the humidity barely tolerable but infinitely better than being outdoors. I soon discovered that the owner had sleeping rooms for rent above the bar, so I paid him for one for the next few days. I knew then that I needed a break before reporting back to my unit. I wasn't authorized the time in transit, but I didn't really care. I only knew that I had to work this crap I was feeling out of my system before reporting in. There was no place for it when leading others out on a patrol. In my present state of mind, I would be no good to myself or to the men who would follow me.

Over the next five days, I passed some time talking with several of the pretty Vietnamese girls working the bar, but I spent a lot more of my time drinking Vietnamese beer and mulling over my predicament. My room was not well-furnished, with only a bed, a wooden chair, a sink and a mirror. There were a couple of clean but dingy grey sheets and a pair of pillows on the bed. The bathroom was down the hall and was shared by the occupants of all the rooms on the floor. There was a single window in my room that looked down on the street in front of the bar. It was open when I entered the room, so I never bothered to close it during the remainder of my stay.

I had gone down to the bar on the first day and asked the manager for a fan. He reluctantly gave me one and it helped a lot. At night, I would lay on the bed and listen to the noise of traffic, the laughter and conversations of people passing by, and the 'krump, krump' of distant explosions. In Vietnam one could always hear the sounds of war going on somewhere.

Lying back with my arms folded behind my head, I asked myself: 'What in the hell are you doing here? You didn't have to come back to Nam. You knew that you could have gotten a medical profile and gone home to Mom and Dad.'

I drank and pondered these thoughts for five days; then it hit me like an RPG round. I finally realized that I belonged here. This was my generation's war. I still had a job to do. My mission was not yet complete. The enemy had killed Bellwood and shot up my team. I needed to get some pay-back or I'd never be able to forgive myself.

The next day I gathered my belongings and took another pedicab back to the air base. When I got to the terminal building, I called my unit at Dong Tam. The company clerk answered the phone. When I told him who it was, he said: 'Sergeant Thayer, where in the hell have you been? We got orders on you a week ago.' I told him that I was at the air base in Saigon waiting for a flight to Dong Tam. He told me that I needed to report in as quickly as I could; Captain Dickey wanted to talk to me. Before I could respond, Captain Dickey was on the phone and said: 'Thayer, where the hell are you?' I told him the same thing I had told the clerk: that I was at Tan Son Nhut Air Base trying to get a lift back to the company. He said to wait there; he would send a chopper to get me and that he would meet me at the helipad at Dong Tam when I arrived.

An hour later, the Huey touched down at the 9th Division's main base camp. True to his word, Captain Dickey, his driver and my two PRUs were there waiting for me. My two Vietnamese teammates greeted me with several bear hugs and back pats. It was good to see them, too. Captain Dickey ordered everyone to mount up and we headed back to the Ranger area a short distance away.

When we reached the company area, Captain Dickey told me that I would be sharing a hooch with Staff Sergeant Frost. I knew Frost.

He was a good man and a great team leader. He was a big guy, at least 6ft 2in. He had short red hair and a large red mustache. He kind of reminded me of Sergeant Peacock in the film *The Devil's Brigade*. I told Captain Dickey that sharing a room with Frost was fine with me. I was shocked that the CO never once mentioned or questioned me about my week-long absence.

I checked in with the company clerk, dropped off my records, then went to see the Supply Sergeant. I told him that I had no idea what had happened to my M16 after I got to the hospital and they shipped me out to Japan. He shook his head and told me not to worry about it; that he would take care of it.

I then drew new camo fatigues, web gear, canteens, grenades, poncho, twenty magazines, a couple of bandoliers of ammo, a compass and a CAR-15. I loaded up everything and headed to my room. Frosty was there when I walked in and dropped my gear on the extra bunk. He looked up and said: 'Hey, Thayer, good to see you. You'll have to tell me about your extended R&R in Japan.' He laughed heartily, which made his crimson mustache flare back against his ruddy cheeks.

He had the room fixed up really nicely; at least, that is, for a room in the middle of a war zone. There was a large American flag hanging on the wall, several pin-up photos of some very pretty girls, two beds (one on each side of the room), an AM/FM radio, a small electric refrigerator, a double-burner hot plate and a nice large table fan. There were shelves on the end wall loaded with canned goods, crackers and packets of LRRP rations. In addition, there was a large bottle of Jack Daniels that Frosty quickly pointed out was off-limits to unauthorized personnel, then laughed and told me not to worry, he would share it with me.

Chapter Twenty-Six

The day after my return to the company, Captain Dickey sought me out and told me that a team was going outside the perimeter of Dong Tam for a short recon patrol. He asked if I wanted to tag along to get my 'feet wet'. It had been nearly two months since my last patrol, and it had been a bad one. Captain Dickey was aware that anyone who had gone through what I had just been through needed to walk again before he tried to run. I understood immediately where he was coming from and agreed that it was probably a good idea for me to go out on a humbug patrol to get the cobwebs out. I told him that I would appreciate tagging along with the team and left to get my gear set up and ready for the mission.

An hour later, we walked through the main gate and angled away toward our recon area. We proceeded slowly which was our nature on patrol and kept our eyes on a patch of trees a couple of hundred meters from the Dong Tam perimeter. Just as we reached the cover of the trees, our point man hit a trip-wire hidden in the vegetation. We all heard the cap pop in the Chicom frag and dove to the ground. A couple of seconds later the grenade detonated, sending shrapnel up and out from the point of the explosion.

After the echo of the blast had died out, we slowly rose to our feet and started checking ourselves for wounds. Amazingly, no one had been hit. God had smiled on us that day, that was for certain. It was a reality check for me, reminding me that the war was not a game to be taken lightly. However, I couldn't help but make fun of our good fortune, blurting out: 'Damn, guys, I just got back to the company. Couldn't you have waited a while to break me in?' Despite the close call, my comment caused a round of laughter among my teammates.

Two hours later, a member of our patrol flushed a pig out of another tree-line and shot it. We cut an 8ft bamboo pole, tied its feet together, and thrust the pole through its legs to carry it back to the company. There was going to be a barbecue this evening in the Ranger company area.

About that time a white-haired Vietnamese elder came out of a nearby hut mad as hell. We had obviously shot his pig and he was demanding justice. Our team leader listened patiently to his rants for several minutes, not understanding a single word he was saying, but the old man's gestures and tone of voice convinced all of us that this needed to be settled on site. The team leader finally decided to take up a collection among the members of the patrol and offer the old-timer a cash settlement that was probably four times what the pig was worth. Satisfied that he wasn't going to file a complaint with the province chief, we shouldered our booty and headed back to the main gate. The patrol was over.

That evening after we had dressed out and butchered the pig, we had a fantastic barbecue for everyone who was in the company area. It was infrequent that we got to do something that managed to take our collective minds off the war. This was one of those instances. The barbecue pork, cold beer and a few hours of light-hearted laughter and camaraderie were just what the doctor had ordered. I was back among my peers and everything was as it should be.

Chapter Twenty-Seven

Two days later, Captain Dickey sent a runner to my room and told me to come to the orderly room. When I got there, he announced that a deuce and a half truck was going to make a run to Tan An and he wanted me to be on it. I told him 'Yes, Sir,' and went to round up my PRUs. Frosty asked where I was going when I went to our room to grab my gear, so I told him we were heading out to Tan An and that I would see him soon.

We piled into the back of the deuce and a half, lined our gear up in the center of the bed and sat down on the rough wooden fold-down bench seats on either side. I had Bao and Dien with me, and the rest of the team would be waiting for me at Tan An. There were a couple of old hands returning from R&R and three cherries on their way to join up with the 3rd Brigade. They would be sharing the ride with us.

On the way to Tan An, we passed a slow-moving bus. One of the infantry guys tossed a smoke grenade into one of the open windows as we passed the bus. In seconds, the bus slammed to a stop, purple smoke pouring from every opening in the vehicle. People scampered out of the doors and windows, running in all directions. It was not a very humanitarian thing to do, but the results were as funny as all get out. I guessed that was why they referred to us as the 'Ugly Americans'. To those of us in the back of the truck it was only meant as a teenage prank, not intended to cause harm or injury. To the Vietnamese civilians on the bus it was another reason for them to hate us.

We arrived at Tan An early in the afternoon. I checked in with the new platoon leader, First Lieutenant Zapata, to let him know that we had arrived. He looked us over and said: 'Well, Sergeant Thayer, you have some new members on your team.' He introduced me to the new LRPs who had been assigned to Tango 1-1. 'Sergeant, this is Sef Gallardo, Chris Valenti, and Mike Volheim. I believe you already know Willy Boone.'

After shaking hands all round, the officer smiled at me and said: 'We're glad to have your team operational again, Sergeant Thayer. Things have been going pretty hot and heavy the past two weeks.' I nodded and asked him if he knew how Lieutenant Hill was doing. Shortly after I had been wounded and was in the hospital in Japan, Lieutenant Hill had been badly wounded and shipped back to the States. He had been a fine officer and would be missed.

After we settled in, I had the pleasure of meeting Staff Sergeant Jimmy Booth. He was an older soldier who had been in the Army for several years. The two of us hit it off instantly and became good friends, but one day, not long after that, the lieutenant called for a platoon formation. Jimmy walked into the barracks to make certain everyone got the word. While he was standing there, hands on his hips, he said to me rather curtly: 'You fall in with the others.' I said: 'Hey, wait a minute, Jimmy. We're both staff sergeants.' He fired back: 'No, I outrank you because I got time in grade over you.'

This went on for the next five or six minutes, growing louder and more heated by the second, until Lieutenant Zapata heard the commotion and came out of the Orderly Room to break up our fun.

Staff Sergeant Jim Thayer with his CAR 15 before a night mission.

The author, barefoot, eating a meal with his PRUs (Provincial Reconnaissance Unit) -Dien and Bao, with Sef Galardo and Chris Valenti in the background.

A heavily-armed Huey Gunship carrying a rocket pod, minigun, and M-60 machine gun for fire support. The lives of LRPs were saved more than once by the firepower of these gunships.

Staff Sergeant Jim Thayer.

Rangers dismount from a Huey chopper. (*C.R. Mathis*)

With the jungle right at the water's edge, these narrow canals were prime ambush locations. A sampan is just visible on the right bank.

The author was sitting in front of the twin .50 machine guns on the front of a patrol boat when the gunner opened fire, deafening Thayer for a week.

LRRP

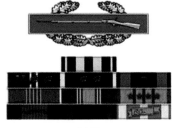

Staff Sergeant Jim Thayer's awards including the Silver Star and Purple Heart awarded for the combat on January 25, 1969 when his patrol came in contact with 150 North Vietnamese Regulars.

25 January 1969: Major General Julian Ewell decorating the author with Silver Star and Purple Heart, plus promotion.

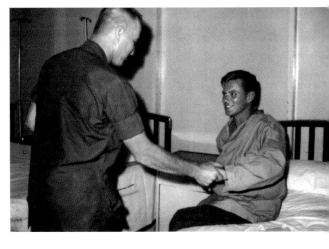

Staff Sergeant Jim Thayer, wounded on 12 June 1969, with Lieutenant Bill Anderson on the right. They are standing in Anderson's room in front of a trophy wall with an AK-47, ammunition bandoleer, and Viet Cong flag.

C.R. Mathis, wounded in 1968. During a firefight, he went back for another team member and was hit in the arm and hand. The wounds were serious enough that he was medevaced home.

Map of combat area, 25 January 1969.

iagram from *Old Reliable* Newspaper, February 5, 1969

Thayer and Hendricks escorting three POWs to a waiting patrol boat. The Viet Cong were captured without a shot being fired.

Above left: Thayer and his PRUs Bao and Dien joking for the camera. Thayer is once again barefoot, often going out on missions without boots.

Above right: Thayer and Zapata before a mission. Thayer modified his CAR 15 by replacing the standard stock with one from a M-16. It slowed the rate of fire allowing for greater accuracy.

Team members Fred Meyers (on the right) and Mike Day wearing a PRC 25 radio on his back.

Above left: Jim Thayer in river. Thayer is holding a M-16 modified with a M-203 grenade launcher attached. He would carry between 10 and 15 grenades when going out on a mission.

Above top right: Sand-filled barrels used to create a berm for perimeter defense at Tan Am.

Above right: Chris Valenti and Thayer before a mission. Camo paint was almost always worn when going out.

Above left: Thayer kitted out for a mission with his modified CAR 15.

Above right: Thayer holding a WW2 era M1 carbine with a 30 round clip. During his time in Vietnam, Thayer would experiment with different weapons including shotguns depending on what the mission was.

Staff Sergeant Jim Thayer enjoying himself at USO show in December 1968.

Left to right: Sef Gallardo, Chris Valenti, Jim Thayer. Cammed-up before a mission. The enemy were scared of the soldiers who wore war paint, knowing them to be especially lethal.

Chapter Twenty-Eight

A day after I returned to Tan An, some of the guys pulled me aside to tell me about the mission back in February when Lieutenant Hill and fourteen other Rangers had been wounded. On 25 February Lieutenant Hill took three teams, totaling twenty Rangers, on a hunter/killer operation into Snoopy's Nose. Snoopy's Nose was a thick jungled area on a tributary river upstream from where it emptied into the Mekong north-west of Dong Tam. It had been given its name because of its shape. It was the land inside a large loop in the secondary waterway that on a map resembled the rounded muzzle of that legendary Peanuts character. It was a nasty place to conduct missions because of the dense vegetation and thick forests, but primarily because of the numerous VC who called it 'home'. Next to VC Island, it was one of the most dangerous locations in the 9th Division Rangers' Area of Operations.

Lieutenant Hill planned to take three teams into the area, with the lead team designated as the hunter/killer team and the other two teams flanking the lead team as support elements. The twenty Rangers were inserted at 1500 hours by three Huey slicks simultaneously touching down in a small three-ship LZ on the east side of the river. They quickly formed up and moved into a dense jungled area about 100 meters from the river. The hunter/killer team, led by Staff Sergeant Ron Wilson, moved into the lead position with the remaining two teams falling in behind. Lieutenant Hill, the mission commander, joined the second team to place himself in the center of the column where he could best control the operation.

Shortly after entering the jungle, the rear security man in the rear team spotted a trail watcher following the column 40 meters back. He immediately took the VC under fire but missed him. The man quickly disappeared in the thick cover. Knowing that they were now compromised, Lieutenant Hill signaled for the lead team to move on but to remain on high alert.

The column continued through the dense forest for another 100 meters before the lead team broke out of the cover and into a small clearing. They stopped there to wait for the other two elements to close up with them. Minutes later, the team saw four VC break out of the jungle on the other side of the clearing less than 50 meters away. The six Rangers of the hunter/killer team immediately opened fire on the VC, killing the first three before the enemy had time to respond, but the last VC disappeared back into the trees before they had a chance to take him down.

By that time, the other two teams closed in on the rear of the lead team to find out what was happening, resulting in all twenty rangers jammed up close together at the edge of the jungle. At that moment, the Rangers heard the unmistakable 'toop' of an M79 grenade-launcher being fired from the jungle on the other side of the clearing. The high-explosive round impacted seconds later just to the left of the massed Rangers, wounding several men. Lieutenant Hill, hit in the ankle, went down immediately. Sergeant Warren Lizzote, standing close to the officer, was hit in the head and collapsed. Several other Rangers suffered minor shrapnel wounds. Before they had a chance to respond, a second round impacted nearby wounding even more Rangers, some for the second time. Lieutenant Hill was one of those hit again, this time just above his left temple. In great pain and unable to stand, the officer heard a third round being fired from the jungle across the clearing. He rolled to his right into a ditch just in time to hear the round explode in the top of a palm tree just above his head, showering the Rangers with shrapnel from the airburst. Hill felt the sharp impact of shrapnel slamming into his back near his left kidney. The pain was unbearable, and he thought for a moment that he was about to die.

Fortunately, the VC grenadier either ran out of ammo or decided it was a good time to flee, as no more rounds were fired into the Rangers' position, but the damage had been done. Fifteen Rangers had been wounded. Only five remained untouched. The survivors immediately set up security and began treating the wounded. Most of the injured had suffered non-life-threatening wounds. However, Hill and Lizzote were both badly injured, with Lizzote unconscious.

Ron Wilson immediately radioed for medevac helicopters and reinforcements before turning his attention back to the wounded. He had a mess on his hands with 75 percent of the patrol down.

The first medevac arrived on station a short time later and tried to set down in the clearing in front of the team, but several failed attempts convinced the pilot that the opening was too tight for the aircraft to touch down. It was late in the day and the sun was beginning to set, which may have contributed to the pilot's inability to land in the clearing. Instead, he lifted out and quickly located another larger, more open area 100 meters away and landed there. He radioed the Rangers his position and told them to start moving the wounded to his location. He was on the deck and waiting.

It was now fully dark. The Rangers shot an azimuth to the waiting medevac and began carrying the more seriously injured through the jungle to its location. It was insanely risky for the medevac crew to wait on the ground at night in 'Indian country' but they did it willingly.

The Rangers got the first batch of wounded loaded on the medevac aircraft and signaled for it to move out, only to discover that the ship was overloaded and could not achieve lift. They were forced to pull off one of the wounded men to allow the ship to get airborne.

The Rangers returned to the remainder of their injured comrades and were preparing to move them back to the clearing in anticipation of a second medevac, only to discover that a 9th Division slick had arrived on the scene and radioed that it was going to attempt to set down in the clearing where the Rangers had taken fire. The Rangers used strobe lights to mark the LZ for the daring pilot. As the aircraft began to settle into the clearing, the tail rotor struck a thick limb on a tree bordering the LZ, causing the Huey to lose control and crash to the ground. Although the impact was substantial, none of the aircrew was injured. With the downed bird blocking the clearing, there was no chance of another helicopter being able to land there.

The Rangers were instructed to get the rest of the wounded to the secondary LZ. Another medevac was inbound. A short time later, the last of the wounded were placed aboard the medevac and the five uninjured Rangers moved back into the jungle to rejoin the aircrew at the crash site. They knew that they would have to set up security and remain with the downed aircraft until they could be reinforced and the ship recovered.

Back at Tan An the 3rd Brigade Commander had been informed of the catastrophe at Snoopy's Nose. When he discovered that the Rangers had been wounded by an M79 in the hands of an enemy soldier, he was irate. Two weeks earlier, one of his platoons had been ambushed by a large VC unit. A grenadier had been killed, and before his body could be recovered, the enemy had moved in to strip him of his weapon and ammo. The colonel was adamant that his troops recover that weapon. He believed that it had been the one used on the Ranger element in Snoopy's Nose. He contacted one of his battalion commanders, Lieutenant Colonel David Hackworth, and told him that the Brigade had a 'mess on its hands'. He ordered Hackworth to 'handle it'.

A short time later, an LOH scout helicopter arrived at the crash site and hovered near the edge of the clearing. Colonel Hackworth, dropped to the ground, linked up with the five remaining Rangers and the four-man helicopter crew. He took charge of the situation and set up security around the downed Huey until morning when a Chinook helicopter arrived to recover it. Only then were Hackworth, the Rangers and the aircrew extracted.

The two medevacs had flown the wounded directly to the 3rd Surgical Center at Dong Tam. They were rushed into triage where the seriously wounded were taken immediately into surgery, while the lesser wounded were treated there and released. Lieutenant Hill had been wounded three separate times and had lost a lot of blood from the wound in his back. He was immediately taken into X-ray where it was discovered that a grenade fragment had lodged in his vena cava. It was life-threatening, so he was immediately rushed into surgery where the fragment was successfully removed. The shrapnel in his ankle and the piece above his temple were left in place. His leg was put in a cast, then he was assigned to the recovery ward there at Dong Tam. He remained at the 3rd Surgical Center for the next two days. Although he had lost a lot of blood and was in a weakened state, he was not given transfusions at Dong Tam. On the third day, he was airlifted by C-7 Caribou to Can Tho where he was finally given the life-saving blood transfusions. Lieutenant Hill remained there for a week recovering some of his strength before being shipped to Japan and finally back to the States.

Robert Hill was an outstanding officer. He looked out for his men and led from the front. He would be missed by me and all the Rangers he led.

Chapter Twenty-Nine

Mike O'Day was still in the company but was no longer going out on patrols. Instead, he had been assigned to our radio relay team out of Tan An. He'd been an excellent ATL for me, but I understood that he was 'short' and had been given a position on the relay team to keep him out of the bush until he rotated back to the States. I'm sure that the January 25th mission had also served to take some of the wind out of his sails. It had achieved a lasting impact on all of us who had survived it. While my team was on stand-down, I decided to go out to an ARVN outpost with Mike to keep him company while he was serving on radio relay duty. We spent the entire night on a bunker talking about what we wanted to do when we got home.

Mike had been a great soldier and a true warrior, but I could tell that he had had enough of the war. Like many young men who sacrifice their youth, their spirit and their humanity in battle to slay their fellow man without mercy, Mike had paid a heavy price. He had earned the opportunity for a cool-down during his last month in-country. No one would begrudge him that. The war had turned many enthusiastic young men into angry old men. You could never recover that lost innocence of youth. It was gone forever. Generations of warriors dating back to the ancient world had likely shared this same experience. I would imagine that it will be the same for future generations until mankind finds a way to truly achieve permanent peace…or destroys itself and the world we live in.

I returned to Tan An early the next day, thankful for the opportunity to have spent some special time with Mike. I hoped it was as good for him as it had been for me. I learned that every warrior had his limits. No one could do this kind of work forever and remain sane. You had to recognize when you reached that point of no return. Crossing it was the end of one's humanity. After talking with Mike, I sensed that I hadn't reached that point yet, but I knew it was drawing near. I was still ready and willing to take the war to the enemy.

Chapter Thirty

I got my new team together on 23 March and was given a mission to pull a recon sweep around the perimeter of Tan An. We saddled up and headed out to the main gate to start our patrol.

We were about 700 meters outside the perimeter wire with the tree-line between us and Tan An when I spotted a VC wading across a shallow rice paddy 100 meters away. Without giving the matter a second thought, I took off in a dead sprint after him, hoping to capture him for interrogation. I managed to gain 20 meters on him before he heard the splashing and turned to see this big American Ranger coming at him, huffing and puffing like a charging water buffalo.

The slender VC hesitated for perhaps two seconds before he kicked on the afterburners and left me far behind. I pursued him for another 50 meters before coming to a full stop and stood there watching him disappear into the next tree-line. I was forced to acknowledge a valuable lesson. A 180lb Ranger, wearing web gear, carrying a rifle and clad in jungle boots, had about as much of a chance of running down a wiry 100lb VC carrying only a rifle and wearing nothing on his feet as a giant sloth has in catching a gazelle. It was indeed a painful lesson, but a lesson from which I would learn. It suddenly struck me that if Charlie can run around the Delta barefoot, why can't Jimmy Thayer do the same? On many future patrols in the swamps and rice paddies of the Delta I would leave my boots behind while on patrol. I would tape my pant legs tight above my ankles with 'high-speed' tape to keep the leeches away from the family jewels, and just 'go native'. It didn't take long for the soles of my feet to toughen enough to the point where the gumbo and muck actually felt good against my bare skin. However, there were also times at night while on patrol that I would have to shove my bare feet down in the mud to keep the leeches and mosquitoes from feasting on my exposed flesh.

CHAPTER THIRTY

My teammates probably thought I had been out in the sun too long, but I was confident that no VC would ever out-run this child again.

This was also the point in my tour where I managed to get myself in a very bad routine. I'm not certain that it was bad for me, but I don't think it was the best situation in which to build team morale and cohesion. I would run a mission, return to Tan An, take a quick shower, put on a clean set of tiger fatigues, grab my CAR-15 or a British Sterling 9mm and head for Saigon. I would go directly to the same bar I had discovered on my return to Vietnam from Camp Zama, Japan. I'd rent a room over the bar, hang out downstairs talking to the girls and drinking Vietnamese beer, and after a day or two, I'd catch a ride back to Tan An to pull another mission. Rides to and from Tan An were never difficult to find. There was always a truck or jeep headed back and forth between Tan An and Saigon. None of the guys on my team or the other Rangers in the Company ever said anything about my trips to Saigon, but I knew that it had to bother them. I was in a very bad place, yet I could not bring myself to change.

The MPs manning the check station at the outskirts of Saigon got to know me after my first two or three trips. The first time I bugged out for the city, one of them said to me: 'Hey, Sarge, you know that area you want to go to is off limits to GIs?' I just stood there ignoring him and fingering my weapon until he said: 'Well, you be careful and stay out of trouble.'

After a while, it got to the point where they would just smile and wave me through. On my fourth trip to Saigon, I was standing there talking to one of the MPs and another one on the other side of the highway checking vehicles yelled: 'Hey, Sarge, I got you a ride to your favorite bar. Hurry up and get over here.'

I said goodbye to the MP I was chatting with and started striding across the macadam highway when two Vietnamese 'cowboys' on a motor cycle smashed into my right thigh, spinning me around like a top. Fortunately for me, I kept my balance and didn't go down, but the two Vietnamese on the bike were not so lucky. The bike cartwheeled, tossing the two young men across the hard-surface road. The MP who had gotten me the ride hollered: 'Are you okay, Sarge? I never seen anything like that before. Two guys on a speeding bike can't knock down a single Ranger. You dudes must be tough as nails.' He laughed and shook his head in disbelief.

I didn't say anything. I just stood there rubbing my badly bruised leg, trying to act like I did this kind of crap every day. After the initial pain subsided and a dull ache took its place, I gimped over to the three-quarter-ton truck and climbed in the passenger seat to catch a ride to Saigon. The two young Vietnamese had suffered some nasty scrapes and abrasions and were very slow to recover. They finally managed to get back to their feet and walked over to look at their badly damaged motor bike.

When I got to the bar, several of the Vietnamese bar girls asked me why I was limping. When I told them what had happened to me, they hurried away and soon returned with some ice wrapped in a bar towel to serve as a compress on the swelling in my leg. I didn't know if it was the ice, the beer or the attention from a bevy of pretty young girls that made the pain ease up, but after a few hours I had managed to all but forget about my recent traffic accident.

Chapter Thirty-One

On 26 March we received notice that we'd be going out that day to try to grab a prisoner for S-2. I decided this time to take out a five-man team to accomplish the snatch. I selected Valenti, Volheim and my two PRUs, Bao and Dien, to join me on the patrol. I also made the decision that this would be one of those times I would leave my boots behind and go barefoot. Knowing what the terrain was like in this AO, I knew that jungle boots would only prove a hindrance. I could sense that the other two Americans on the team were thinking that their team leader had lost his mind by going native, but my PRUs patted me on the back and smiled approvingly.

Lieutenant Zapata told us in the pre-mission briefing that there was a village about 5 klicks out from Tan An where S-2 had been receiving agent reports of heavy enemy activity. It could very easily prove to be a good place for a quick in-and-out prisoner snatch.

I selected a spot on the map that appeared open enough for a helicopter to sneak in and drop us off, yet far enough away from the village to avoid detection by its inhabitants. The five of us hurried to the helipad to meet our lift ship. While my teammates were boarding, I passed the coordinates of our LZ to the pilot.

The Huey flew nap of the earth all the way out to the AO to throw off enemy spotters. It slowed momentarily 5ft above the clearing I had selected on my map, and we jumped from the skids into a field of elephant grass that was no more than a meter high.

We moved out through the grass into a large grove of banana trees and 'went ghost' for several minutes to observe the area around us. I wanted to make sure that our insertion had not drawn the attention of the villagers less than 600 meters away. As I dropped to one knee in the underbrush to diminish my silhouette, I put my left hand on the ground to brace myself. It was at that moment that I spotted the

light green form of a deadly bamboo viper sliding out between my
index and second fingers. For some strange reason, the serpent had
chosen to flee instead of striking. The bamboo viper, also known as the
'two-stepper' for the speed with which its venom kills, is one of the
most poisonous snakes in Indo-China. Once again, I had managed to
cheat death by the narrowest of margins. My guardian spirit was still
watching over me. However, the close call with the viper convinced me
that it was time to move out of the banana grove, perhaps a little sooner
than I had planned.

After putting a safe distance between ourselves and the trees, we
found some very heavy underbrush beneath a wooded area made up
of coconut trees, large nipa palms and a few banana trees. Since it was
running in the direction of the village, I decided that we would use the
cover of the trees to get within range of our target. I checked my map
and determined that the village was less than 500 meters north of our
present location. We needed to get close enough to observe it without
being spotted ourselves.

After moving less than 30 meters through the heavy cover, I grew
concerned over the noise we were making and the noticeable back trail
we were leaving in our passing. Suddenly, we broke out of the underbrush
onto a wide, well-used trail heading directly toward the village. I decided
to back away from the trail about 10 meters, then flank it for as long as
it continued to run in the direction we needed to go.

We followed the high-speed trail for nearly 300 meters when the point
man held up his hand to stop the team. He signaled that someone was
coming up the trail toward us. We froze in place and watched to see if the
man was alone or if he was the point element for a larger unit. I let him
walk past our position, then turned to check him out from behind. He
was alone and armed with an American-made .30 caliber M1 carbine.
He was also wearing a Chicom web belt with several magazine pouches
around his waist.

When he was 30 meters past our position, I gave the signal that he
was our guy. I motioned for the team to follow me, then took off at a
dead run to catch up to the VC. He must have heard me charging down
the trail because he suddenly took off, running at full speed, but this time
the advantage was mine. He was wearing Ho Chi Minh sandals and I was
the one who was barefoot. I caught up to him after a chase of less than
40 meters. Grabbing the back of his shirt at the neck, I did a horse-collar

take-down of the enemy soldier. If I had been an NFL linebacker, I'd have surely gotten a 15-yard penalty for that tackle.

While I held the VC down, Bao jumped in and grabbed his carbine and web gear while Valenti bound his hands behind him and gagged him with a strip of cloth. Satisfied that the POW was secure, we jerked him to his feet and took him with us as we moved out through the underbrush.

A couple of hundred meters south I stopped the team and radioed Operations to tell them we had a prisoner and requested an immediate extraction. I gave them the coordinates of an open area 50 meters to our west and told them we would pop smoke to mark the LZ when we heard the chopper.

A short time later, the Huey arrived on site and landed next to our smoke. We tossed the POW aboard and climbed in quickly behind him. It had been a short but successful mission and the team had performed brilliantly.

After we turned over our POW to the appreciative people at S-2, we went back to our barracks. Naturally, Volheim and Valenti couldn't wait to tell Jimmy Booth and the rest of the Rangers about my narrow escape from the deadly viper. Not surprisingly, my teammates greatly embellished my performance in cheating death once again. No matter what they said, I have never once in my life done a double-backward somersault!

Chapter Thirty-Two

While Tango 1-1 was capturing a prisoner outside of Tan An, Captain Dickey took a five-man team into War Zone D to locate and follow a trail complex that was suspected of being heavily used by VC operating in and out of Cambodia. War Zone D was a dangerous place to patrol. It was an enemy sanctuary area sitting on the border between South Vietnam and Cambodia and was well-protected by large numbers of VC and NVA. Prior incursions into the area by US and RVN forces had proven costly.

Captain Dickey's team inserted at last light on 27 March and set up for the night in a dense stand of brush 200 meters off the LZ. The next morning, the team moved out into a thick wooded area and immediately encountered a high-speed trail running west to east. It was wide enough for two men to walk down side by side and showed recent heavy use. The team backed off into the jungle and paralleled the trail for the next two hours, before reaching a spot where the trail split, with one segment heading to the south-west and the other segment continuing due west. Just before reaching the Y in the trail, a tree had fallen across it, making that section of trail impassable. Dickey decided that it was a good spot to set up an OP, since any enemy soldiers would have to come to a stop when they reached the deadfall. The Rangers would watch the trail at that location for the remainder of the day.

It was nearly 1600 hours when the team spotted three armed VC moving down the main trail from the east. When the enemy soldiers reached the roadblock formed by the downed tree, they came to a stop. The Rangers observed that one of the VC was very short and thin, another was medium-sized and rather well-built, while the third was tall and rather fat for a Vietnamese, reminding Dickey and his fellow teammates of a Buddha. While the five Rangers continued to watch the trio, the short, skinny VC got down on his hands and knees and crawled under the deadfall. Safe on the other side, he turned to his companions and exhorted them to come across. Hesitating for only a moment, the medium-sized VC slung his SKS carbine over his shoulder and climbed up and over the downed tree, joining the little guy on the other side. Now the first two began chiding the fat VC to come across so that they could get on with their journey. He stood there appraising the situation, but refused to cross. The good-natured teasing went on for several minutes to no avail.

After a while, the first two enemy soldiers had had enough of their companion's reluctance to even attempt a crossing. They began to berate him, growing angrier by the minute. Finally, the porcine VC moved up to the deadfall and began to climb over it. His two companions began laughing at his efforts, which grew even funnier when the man got one leg over the main trunk, then hooked the back of his shorts on a broken limb before he could bring his other leg over. His comrades began laughing aloud at his predicament.

Back in the brush, the five Rangers had to stifle their own laughter at the spectacle developing in front of them. For a moment, they forgot that the three men were armed enemy soldiers. About that time, the chubby VC tried to force his other leg over the trunk of the fallen tree, only to have his shorts, still hung up on the broken limb, ripped down to expose his bare but ample bottom.

The other two VC began laughing loudly and pointing at their now embarrassed comrade, riding him unmercifully. It was too much for the Rangers, as one of them broke out in a loud guffaw. The fat was now in the fire. As the first two VC heard the laughter back in the brush, they turned around, grabbing at the weapons slung over their shoulders. The Rangers had no choice. The point man and Captain Dickey, both carrying silenced Sterling submachine guns, opened fire, killing the three VC instantly.

The Rangers retrieved the enemy soldiers' weapons and checked the bodies for documents, then slipped back into the jungle and away from the trail. They moved several hundred meters to the east and set up for the night in a thick patch of jungle not far from a clearing.

The next morning, Dickey called for an extraction. Killing the three VC the day before had compromised the team. When their bodies were discovered, and there was no doubt they would be, every VC and NVA in War Zone D would know that an American patrol was operating in the area. It wouldn't take long for the enemy to be hunting them. Remaining there any longer would only be asking for trouble.

On the flight back to Dong Tam, Dickey felt saddened about killing the three enemy soldiers. Watching their antics and how they reacted with each other back at the Y in the trail made them seem…well…just like ordinary people and not the enemy.

Chapter Thirty-Three

Tango 1-1 drew the ultimate dream mission on 1 April, April Fool's Day. Intelligence had reported that an NVA general would be overseeing a troop and supply build-up near a village north-west of Tan An. The lieutenant told me to get my team ready for a snatch-and-grab mission. If the Intel was accurate, we were to locate and capture the officer and bring him in for interrogation. This could be a major Intel coup for our side if my team could pull it off.

I decided to go in 'light' with only a five-man team: web gear, weapons and full camo. Chris Valenti would be my ATL on the mission and Mike Volheim my RTO. I would also once again be taking my two PRUs. If we needed a translator, they would be invaluable.

After the pre-mission briefing where we got the coordinates of the village, Lieutenant Zapata wished us good luck and we made our way to the nearby helipad to board our waiting Huey. I pulled out my map and showed the pilot the spot I had selected for our insertion, then we all mounted the aircraft for the flight out to our AO (Area of Operations).

Ten minutes later, the Huey slick lost altitude, indicating that it had reached the location I had selected for our LZ. It slowed its forward momentum just enough for us to be able to leap to the ground into a wide expanse of elephant grass. The grass proved to be no more than 3ft high, which made our drop to the ground about 5ft. Squatting in the sparse cover until the aircraft had cleared the area and had moved out of sight, we hesitated only long enough to make sure our arrival had not drawn the attention of any nosy neighbors.

Satisfied that we had not been compromised, I gave the signal for the team to move out. One of the PRUs took point and I moved in behind him in the 'slack' position. Volheim was behind me with the radio, followed by Valenti and the second PRU.

We got out of the elephant grass as fast as we could and entered a thick jungled area. There was a well-used trail running through the heart of it. It was always bad policy to walk on heavily traveled trails, so we paralleled it about 10 meters back in the brush. Any further and we wouldn't have been able to keep the trail in sight. Any closer and anyone using it would have been able to see us.

Twenty minutes later, the jungle started thinning a little and we could make out a village 60 meters ahead of us. People were moving about in and around the structures. We were still in relatively thick cover, so I decided to set up an OP back in the trees to monitor the area for enemy activity. I spread my team out into a security wheel and sat back to watch and wait.

Two hours later we had yet to see anything out of the ordinary. The activity in the village was what you'd expect: children playing, adults going about doing their chores, old men sitting together talking and enjoying a pipe.

Suddenly, a pair of Vietnamese woodcutters walked right up to us. One of them had an ax in his hand and the other was carrying a hand-saw. Their eyes grew as large as saucers when they spotted us squatting in the brush. Their mouths dropped open, then they turned and ran back toward the village.

As soon as the two men disappeared among the huts, a heavy rain began to fall. Realizing that the woodcutters would tell everyone about the 'men with the painted faces' hidden in the woods, I knew we had to get out of the area as quickly as possible. We hurriedly pulled back through the heavy cover, taking advantage of the downpour to cover the sound of our movement.

Satisfied that we had put a safe enough distance between ourselves and the village to allow us a break, we stopped in some thick underbrush and called the radio relay team to tell them we had been compromised and needed an immediate extraction. A few minutes later, they called us back and told us that all aircraft were grounded because of the weather. They advised us to go to ground and become 'ghosts' until the aircraft could fly again.

It was growing dark by then, so we hurriedly put a full klick's distance (1,000 meters) between ourselves and the village. Barely able to see because of the loss of light and the heavy rain, I made the decision at 2100 hours to find some thick cover and hole up in it until dawn. The rain was still coming down hard, so there was no hope of a night extraction.

We located a patch of dense underbrush beneath a cluster of banana trees and crawled into it on our hands and knees. As we were settling in, we could barely make out a string of lights far off in the distance. We watched them through the rain for several minutes, determining that they were still several hundred meters away, but it was also apparent that they were moving slowly in our direction. The two woodcutters had undoubtedly spread the word of our presence, and we were pretty sure that the people behind the lights were not curious villagers.

I ordered my teammates to set out a couple of Claymore mines in the direction of the oncoming lights as we prepared for a fight. I was hoping to avoid contact since we would have no air support to back us up, and it appeared from the number of lights approaching us that we were vastly outnumbered.

By 2230 hours the enemy had moved very close to our hide site. We could hear them talking, even over the sound of the rain. Just before we had moved into our defensive position, I had spotted a canal about 100 meters behind us. I had made the decision then that if we had to run during the night, the canal would serve as our rally point. I whispered to everyone on the team that if the enemy soldiers got any closer, we would blow the Claymores, empty one magazine apiece into them, then break cover and hightail it for the canal to our rear.

Fifteen minutes passed, and the line of flashlights was nearly on top of us. We blew the two Claymores almost simultaneously, stood up in the underbrush and let them have almost 100 rounds of 5.56 caliber ball ammo at close range. As the gunfire petered out, I shouted 'GO!' and turned to run for the canal. We reached it almost together and leaped into it. Fortunately for us, it was shallow and presented no problem in crossing to the other side.

We continued running for another 100 meters but were forced to slow down our flight so that we wouldn't leave anyone behind in the thicker cover. In a flash of lightning I observed that there was a rice paddy just ahead of us. We splashed noisily across it, then dove behind the paddy dike on the far side of it to set up another hasty ambush to hit the enemy again if they were still on our tails.

We lay side by side, our lungs gasping for air, as we waited and watched for any signs of pursuit. It was by now the middle of the night and still raining, but in the occasional flashes of lightning we could still make out some shadowy forms in the hazy darkness.

Ten minutes passed. We saw no more flashlights, nor could we hear anything but the sound of the falling rain. I realized that there was a possibility that the enemy had learned a hard lesson and had decided to continue their search for us without the benefit of illumination. I decided that it was time to change direction to throw off any further pursuit. Without the aid of their lights they wouldn't be able to see our tracks in the muddy ground. I checked my wrist compass and made the decision to head north at right angles to our previous direction of flight.

Giving the signal to move out as quietly as possible, we covered another 300 meters and set up again in a thick palm forest with dense underbrush. We spent the rest of the night at full alert, ready to run again or stand and fight.

After an uneventful night, the morning came on a clear sky, the rain having moved off to the east. We checked our maps to determine our location, then called for an extraction in an open area not far away from our present position. When we heard the Huey approaching, we popped a smoke grenade and tossed it out in the PZ (pick-up zone). As soon as the Huey touched down, we climbed aboard and took our seats for the short ride back to Tan An. We were soaked and chilled to the bone, but we were still alive. To a man, we were just happy to have survived a very tough night and an extremely dangerous situation.

Chapter Thirty-Four

April was starting off with a bang. The same day Tango 1-1 made it back from its April Fool's Day horror show, another E Company (Ranger) mission was getting ready for its own rendezvous with destiny, and the location would be the dreaded Thoi Son Island.

Captain Dickey, the Commanding Officer of E Company (Ranger) decided to go back to 'VC Island' on a snatch-and-grab mission. The island, a Viet Cong stronghold within mortar and rocket distance of Dong Tam, My Tho and the 9th Division base camp, was a thorn in the side of US and ARVN (Army of the Republic of Vietnam) troops operating in the area. Previous missions by 9th Division LRPs had proven that the island was not friendly to invaders.

Captain Dickey decided that a different approach was needed to ensure the success of the mission. The Ranger commander put a plan together and sold it to 9th Division G-3. His plan called for three reinforced Ranger teams to land on the island at low tide in a late-night insertion by Swift boats, followed up by a quick daylight raid into the center of the island to capture and bring out one or more VC prisoners. If it could be accomplished, the mystery of who or what was operating on Thoi Son would be solved.

Dickey selected three five-man Ranger teams stationed at Dong Tam for the mission: Team 2-2, led by Staff Sergeant Paul Cicero; Team 1-7, led by Staff Sergeant Herb 'Frosty' Frost; and Team 1-4, led by Staff Sergeant Joe Boudreaux would make up the operational team. Captain Dickey would go in with the heavy team as the ground commander. First Lieutenant Bill Anderson, Sergeant First Class Julio Dominguez, Sergeant First Class Jesse Stevens and Specialist Fourth Class Bobby Byrne would also join the mission to supplement the fifteen team members. In addition, three PRUs were added at the last minute to serve as interpreters and to provide their uncanny ability to detect enemy booby-traps. Altogether, twenty-three US/RVN troops would make up the task force.

The Rangers planned to go in with a lot more firepower than they normally carried on an operation. There would be a couple of M79 grenade-launchers among the weapons carried on the mission, along with several of the new experimental M203 'over and under' grenade-launchers. One of Team 1-4's Rangers would also be humping an M60 machine gun. Three other members of the team were assigned to carry a couple of belts of 7.62 caliber each to 'feed the pig', as the M60 was affectionately called by American troops serving in Vietnam.

Sergeant Mike Calog had just arrived at E Company the day before the mission. He had volunteered for Rangers after serving three months as a switchboard operations sergeant with the 9th Signal Battalion. It would prove to be a rough initiation into the Rangers for this young NCO.

All personnel attended a pre-mission briefing late in the afternoon, then returned to their barracks to await the call to move to the helipad. Staff Sergeant Cicero called his team together on the second floor of the barracks and talked about how they would operate once they got to the island. Everyone could see that the tough New Yorker was openly nervous about the patrol.

At 2230 hours, word was sent to both barracks buildings that it was time for the teams to mount up and move to the helipad. Three Huey slicks were there waiting for the teams to board. No one spoke a word as they crowded into the open cabins and claimed their spots on the dimpled steel floors. It would be a short ten-minute flight to the docks at My Tho.

It was 2300 hours and there was a full moon when the twenty-three men disembarked from the helicopters and climbed aboard the three waiting Swift boats moored to the docking facilities on the Mekong River at My Tho. Captain Dickey, Lieutenant Anderson and SFCs Dominguez and Stevens boarded the craft designated as the Command and Control boat, while the remainder of the teams divided up and boarded the other two Swift boats.

While Captain Dickey was doing a final head count before stepping up on the deck, he was approached by a man dressed in fatigues but not carrying a weapon. He identified himself as a news correspondent for the ABC Network and told the Ranger officer that the 9th Division Chief of Staff Colonel Hunt had given his approval for him to accompany the

Rangers on the mission. Dickey had already received the order from Colonel Hunt, yet still felt the need to tell the man that it was going to be a very dangerous operation, but the newsman insisted he be allowed to go along. Dickey finally shrugged his shoulders and told him to climb aboard the C&C boat and stay out of the way. He could observe the operation from his perch on the water.

It was nearly midnight when the boats cast off their mooring lines and backed away from the docks, their powerful motors muffled as they moved out into the channel. The Rangers were all standing as close to the bows of the boats as they could get in anticipation of the coming insertion. They could barely make out the dark mass of the huge island on their left as the boats sped up the Mekong River. Dickey had told the lieutenant (junior grade) commanding the C&C boat that he wanted to be inserted approximately at the halfway point on the 7-mile-long island.

Reaching the area of the landing, the three Swift boats approached the shore side-by-side with no more than 15 meters between each boat. As they neared the shore, the noise of their bows scraping against the water plants and aquatic vegetation sounded deafening to the Rangers waiting to insert. Grinding to a stop 10 meters out from the shoreline provided the signal for the twenty-three warriors to drop from the decks of the Swift boats and into the darkened river. Immediately after the decks were cleared, all three boats reversed thrust and withdrew out into the channel.

The twenty Rangers and three PRUs stood shoulder-to-shoulder in the chest-deep water and waited several minutes to make sure their insertion had gone unnoticed. For the 5ft 7in Calog, the water level reached just below his chin. He found himself inching forward, hoping to find a shallower depth. The Rangers had brought a couple of the heavy Starlight scopes with them, and while they waited in the water, the two men with the scopes studied the shoreline for movement. The bright moonlight enhanced the illumination of the first-generation night-vision scopes.

Suddenly, heavy gunfire erupted from the trees back in the shoreline. Green tracers whizzed out over the top of the men standing in the water. Helpless, they could do nothing but fire back, hoping to drive the ambushers away. There was nowhere for them to go. The enemy was to their front and deeper water waited behind them.

They continued to return fire, red and green tracers crossing paths in the moonlight. In less than two minutes the Swift boats were moving back in to recover the helpless troops. The powerful hammering of their six .50 caliber machine guns and their three deck mortars joined the battle and forced the VC to seek cover as the Rangers and their PRU allies grabbed hold of ropes, netting and anything else they could get their hands on as the patrol boats once again reversed thrust and backed out into the channel.

Safely away from the ambush site, the sailors helped pull the waterlogged soldiers back onto the decks of the idling Swift boats. A quick head count revealed that everyone was accounted for. Amazingly, no one had been wounded.

Captain Dickey decided that they would try another insertion further up the island. None of his troops commented when he announced the change of plans. However, the forgotten correspondent stood up from his hiding-place inside the control room and demanded to be taken back to My Tho at once. Dickey looked at him and said: 'You insisted on coming along to see how we operate. You're here for the duration.' The newsman was irate and threatened to sue Dickey and have him court-martialed. Dickey blew off the threat with a shrug of his shoulders and turned away from the terrified civilian. Not willing to accept the Ranger commander's decision, the man turned to the Navy officer standing at the helm and said: 'Take me back to My Tho now.' The Navy lieutenant shook his head and said: 'I'm here to support this operation until it's completed or cancelled. You'll have to wait until it's over.' With that announcement, the frightened man began to cry. He finally gave up and crawled back into the control room to sit glumly down in the corner. There was no fight left in him.

The patrol boats once again surged up the river in a single column. Approximately a mile above the ambush site, the three Swift boats turned on line and moved toward the shore again. In a repeat of the previous insertion, the boats ground to a halt a few meters out from the shore and everyone again slipped over the side and took their positions on line as the boats backed out into the middle of the river.

For the second time, enemy soldiers hidden back in the trees waited until the Swifties had disappeared, then opened fire on the Rangers and PRUs standing silently in the chest-deep river. The battle was brisk as both sides exchanged fire for several minutes until the Swift boats came back in to silence the enemy guns and rescue the beleaguered patrol.

Back on board the boats in the middle of the Mekong River, Captain Dickey was perplexed but far from conceding the night to the enemy. Fortunately, his troops had suffered no casualties in either of their two attempts to land on the island, and except for expending a couple of magazines of ammo apiece, they were good to go. Dickey knew there was no possibility that the VC forces on the island could cover every inch of the shoreline. There had been at least a full squad of enemy soldiers at each of the two ambush sites. It would take an exceptionally large force to cover the entire island with that many troops at each location.

Dickey was not finished yet. Once again, he instructed the naval commander to move another mile and a half up the river and take them in to the island. The young officer nodded, radioed the other two boats and ordered the column to speed up the river to the next location.

The site Dickey picked was near the upper end of the island, not more than a mile from the lights of Dong Tam. The three boats turned left on line and once again approached the darkened shore. The moon was high in the night sky and its muted light glistened on the water as the Swift boats edged into the muddy shoreline.

For the third time in three hours, the Rangers and PRUs slipped from the safety of the large patrol boats and entered the waters of the Mekong River. Shoulder-to-shoulder they moved in a little closer to the shore where the shallower water gave them room to maneuver in case they had to fight again.

All was quiet for several minutes, then the sound of someone or something moving among the trees back from the shore caught their attention. The two Rangers manning the Starlight scopes scanned the tree-line to their front. One of them must have seen something moving because he let the scope hang by its lanyard, swung his weapon around and opened fire at a cluster of vegetation just back from the edge of the water.

Immediately, there was return fire as a heavy volume of green tracers buzzed overhead. It was happening again! The Rangers emptied their magazines into the dark jungle as they backed into the deeper water behind them, seeking protection from the enemy rounds. Again, the Swift boats hastened to their rescue, the heavy .50 calibers tearing into the heavy cover where the VC were hiding. As soon as they reached the stranded soldiers, they waited patiently as the twenty-three men found purchase on the flanks of the boats. They held on with one hand and held their weapons out of the river with the other as the Swift boats backed out into the middle of the river. As the enemy fire petered out, the Navy crewmen moved to help the rapidly tiring Rangers back onto the boats.

Dickey realized that there would be no insertion on the river side of the island. The VC were obviously employing watchers along the bank of the river who alerted squad-sized ambush teams stationed every half-mile or so back from the watchers. These squads would react quickly when the sentries spotted the boats heading toward the shoreline. There could be no other logical explanation.

Suddenly, it occurred to the Ranger commander that there might be a chance that the enemy was not guarding the back side of the island. There were no friendly military bases on the far shore of the Mekong River. The ground was closer to sea level on that side of the island, which would make it tougher to land a shore party. The shoreline was very marshy with thicker vegetation than on the river side of the island. Dickey decided that an insertion on the back side of Thoi Son would more than likely succeed. He ordered the Navy commander to head up-river out of sight and sound of the island, then turn the boats toward the opposite shore and make a silent run down the back side of VC Island. When they reached a point near the lower third of the island, he told the officer to make a run in to the shore and drop them off.

At 0400 hours, the Swift boats made their fourth attempt to deploy the Rangers. They ran into shore, getting as close as they could to the palm trees just inland. The Rangers and their PRUs slipped into the shallow water and sloshed through it into the denser vegetation a few meters back from the river. Unlike the river side of the island, the water continued well back into the palm trees and broadleaf vegetation. There was no solid ground anywhere. They were in a swamp where movement was both labor-intensive and noisy. There was nothing beneath their feet but standing water and gumbo mud that made every step they took a battle with Mother Nature.

About 100 meters in from the river, Dickey signaled the Rangers to form up in a circular perimeter. They would wait out the remaining hours of darkness before moving in toward the center of the island. No one slept while they knelt or squatted in the shin-deep water to await the coming dawn. Mosquitoes and leeches enjoyed the feast.

At 0630, Dickey decided that it was light enough to move out. Putting the three PRUs up at point, the twenty Rangers formed up in a single-file column and waded slowly and silently through the marshy ground, hoping for the opportunity to grab a prisoner or two and get the hell out of there. Progress was slow. Increasing their speed meant making even more noise, and to make more noise was to invite an ambush.

By mid-morning, the ground began to rise and they finally left the marshy terrain behind. They began to encounter well-used footpaths running through the dense brush. Dickey decided that with the PRUs up at point, he would take a chance and walk the footpaths to see where they led. It was not a practice that Rangers normally employed, but twenty-three men breaking through the brush flanking a trail would be heard 100 meters away.

They finally broke out of the brush into a clearing that housed a small hamlet. The column stopped and observed the area for several minutes before determining that it was unoccupied. Dickey signaled the column to move into the hamlet. The point element had just passed the first hooch when someone inside opened fire on the column. Lieutenant Anderson and Sergeant Mike Calog saw several tracers pass between them and dove to the ground. While lying there, they saw Staff Sergeant Cicero leap to his feet, dash past the open door of the hooch, flip a fragmentation grenade over his shoulder into the structure, then do a somersault away from the building. The two Rangers looked at each other regarding the young team leader's remarkable feat and shook their heads in amazement. It was indeed a John Wayne move if they had ever seen one.

As the grenade exploded inside the building, two or three VC opened up on the column from back in the brush beyond the furthest structures. Again, no one was hit in the ambush. As the enemy broke contact and fled, two of the Rangers searched the hooch where the initial gunfire had come from. There was no one inside. While Cicero was making his heroic one-man assault, the VC inside the hut had fled out the back door.

Over the next three hours, the column found three more hamlets. They were all empty. In each, they discovered warm food and cooking fires still burning, but the inhabitants had disappeared. An uncomfortable nervousness began to settle over the soldiers in the task force. The enemy was obviously aware of their presence on the island, making the taking of a POW almost impossible to achieve.

The Rangers encountered several canals and irrigation ditches while they patrolled down the length of the island. The only way to safely cross these obstacles was to use the native 'foot-bridges' that spanned them.

These bridges consisted of a single bamboo pole laid across the span. Most of the poles were approximately 3in in diameter. The barefoot locals had no problem crossing the ditches on these impromptu bridges, but for the larger, heavier American GIs, clad in their unforgiving hard-soled jungle boots, they posed a very difficult challenge. Most of the bridges required two to three giant, well-placed strides to reach the safety of the other side. Success was based on a combination of balance and timing. On the third pole bridge the Rangers had to cross, Sergeant Mike Calog prepared himself for another attempt at defying the pull of gravity. The Ranger took off across the narrow bamboo bridge, his shorter legs turning a three-step crossing into a four. His first three steps were perfect, but just as he neared the opposite bank, his fourth step caught the edge of the pole and sent him slamming into the muddy bank on his knees. Clinging there momentarily while he gathered his thoughts, he looked down to see his right knee was wedged between three 6in-long rusty spike nails that had been driven through a wooden base in a triangular configuration. The spikes had missed impaling his knee on all three points by a mere fraction of an inch. If he had been a bigger man, he would have found out what it was like to be a shish-kabob. As it was, he discovered that he had a long, narrow scratch down the inside of his knee, and on the outside of his knee, his fatigue trousers had been ripped. He had missed a crippling injury by the width of a frog's hair. Pulling his knee cautiously out of the booby-trap, Calog took a hand-up from a couple of Rangers who had crossed the canal just ahead of him. When he looked back down to see how close it had been, he spotted a similar booby-trap on the opposite side of the pole. VC Island was living up to its reputation.

The Rangers had noticed woven fish traps in each of the canals and ditches they had crossed. They had yet to run across even a single rice paddy. They began to wonder how the villagers on Thoi Son Island managed to survive without farming. There had to be rice paddies somewhere on the island, or perhaps the residents were engaged in a heavy amount of trade with the waterborne vendors and merchants who marketed their wares up and down the Mekong River system. Fish alone could not provide a sustainable diet.

Just before noon, one of the Rangers tripped a booby-trap. An American-made pineapple grenade rolled out onto the trail, sending everyone diving for cover. Fortunately, the rusty frag failed to explode.

However, it did manage to heighten the awareness of danger the entire team had felt since their insertion on the island.

By mid-afternoon, Captain Dickey began to doubt the patrol would be able to capture a prisoner. They had yet to see a VC or a civilian inhabitant of the island. It wasn't looking good.

Finally, the point element moved out of a patch of heavy brush and spotted a canal directly in front of them. Squatting over a fish trap down near the waterline was an older Vietnamese man who seemed completely unaware that he was being watched. Suddenly, he looked up to see six heavily camouflaged soldiers peering over the edge of the canal with their weapons pointed directly at him.

Captain Dickey was elated. The old man, who appeared to be in his 50s, was not a VC but he lived on an island that was full of VC. He had to possess some knowledge of the enemy. Dickey decided that he would have to do as far as a prisoner was concerned. The Ranger commander ordered two of his soldiers to get the old man up out of the canal and secure him, while he got on the radio and called for an extraction. Plotting a route back to a point on the back side of the island, he told the Swift boats to pick them up at that location.

On their way to the extraction point the task force began hearing single shots fired in the distance, both to their front and behind them. The VC knew the Americans were on the island and they were signaling each other to keep track of the invaders' position. The Rangers began to feel an increasing sense of urgency to get off the island as soon as possible.

The patrol finally reached the marshy area. Each man realized that they were only a few hundred meters from their extraction point and felt the need to pick up the pace. The column was stretched out with intervals of 5 to 10 meters between each man. It was becoming more and more difficult in the thick muck to keep a constant spacing without making a lot of noise.

The last man in the column was Specialist Fourth Class Florio Chappa. Mike Calog was walking just to his front. Dennis Lastine was a few meters ahead of Calog. As they were drawing closer to the river, Calog stopped to check on Chappa and discovered that he was nowhere in sight. He snapped his fingers several times but got no response in return. Calog turned back to the front to signal Lastine to hold up, but caught sight of him moving into a wall of thick brush 20 meters away. Calog snapped his fingers again, trying to get Lastine's attention, but the Ranger failed to hear him before disappearing through the dense vegetation.

Calog didn't know what to do. He could either catch up to the team or go back for Chappa. Without a moment's hesitation, he turned and went back to find his missing comrade. Calog covered 50 meters down his backtrail before he finally spotted Chappa. The Ranger was a few meters off the trail, mired up to his waist in a pool of thick, sticky mud. The look of utter relief on Chappa's face told Calog that the Ranger had already accepted the fact that he was going to die in that place. As Calog moved to the edge of the mud-pit, he suddenly heard Vietnamese voices on the other side of a wall of dense brush to his left flank. Then he heard more voices and laughter less than 30 meters behind him coming up their backtrail.

He could see from the look of desperation on Chappa's face that he had heard it too. Calog knew he had to do something fast. Holding his rifle in both hands, he braced himself and extended it broadside toward the trapped Ranger. As Chappa grabbed the weapon in both hands, Calog jerked backwards with all his might until he heard the suction pop as he broke the man loose from the grip of the muddy trap.

As the two men rose to their feet, more voices and more laughter could be heard not 15 meters away in the vegetation to their left. They caught the sounds of rounds being jacked into the chambers of multiple weapons. It was time to catch up to their teammates.

They moved out slowly at first, trying not to make any noise, yet fast enough to get ahead to get ahead of both the VC on the flank and the enemy soldiers coming up on their backtrail. They had no doubt that the enemy was trailing them to the shoreline. It occurred to Calog that the enemy might be after the boats.

When the two Rangers decided they had put enough distance between themselves and the VC, they threw caution to the wind and began splashing through the muddy, shallow water toward the river. They finally broke out of the cover onto the shoreline just in time to see the last of the Rangers climbing aboard the waiting Swift boats. Only Staff Sergeant Funk was still in the water up to his waist between two of the boats. He was taking a final head count. When he spotted Chappa and Calog, he shouted: 'Where in the hell have you two been?' Calog answered breathlessly: 'They're right behind us.'

As the three Rangers reached the bow of the closest Swift boat, eager hands reached down to pull them aboard. A big, raw-boned sailor grabbed Calog just as a number of enemy soldiers opened fire on the boats from

CHAPTER THIRTY-FOUR

back in the trees. As soon as Calog was safely aboard, collapsing on the deck next to an equally exhausted Chappa, the big sailor moved back to the deck mortar and began dropping rounds into the dense cover on the shoreline. The .50 calibers quickly engaged the onrushing VC, stopping them dead in their tracks. There was no cover back in the trees strong enough to stop the heavy, armor-piercing rounds.

The three Swift boats backed away from the shore, then turned to speed upstream toward the Dong Tam end of Thoi Son Island. Instead of heading downstream toward My Tho, the Navy commander asked Captain Dickey if he minded if the Rangers stayed aboard for the remainder of the day while the Navy crews carried out their routine patrol work, checking sampans for contraband and weapons. Captain Dickey said that the Rangers wouldn't mind watching the Navy at work while they rested on the decks of the Swift boats and enjoyed the warm sun.

At the end of the day, the Swift boats pulled into the docks at My Tho and dropped off the weary Rangers just in time to board the three Hueys waiting to take them back to Dong Tam. Captain Dickey smiled to himself as a shop-worn war correspondent slipped out the back of the C&C boat and walked away from the dock as fast as his legs could carry him.

That night, the Rangers and their PRUs gathered at the club and enjoyed a few ice-cold beers. They sat around talking until almost midnight, amazed that no one had been wounded or killed during the overnight operation. They were all feeling lucky and very professional, until Sergeant First Class Dominguez stood up and said:

I hate to pop your bubble, boys, but this wasn't nuthin'. When you find yourself on a frozen hill-top in the middle of a Korean winter with a couple thousand Red Chinese charging up the hill at you, falling like dominoes as more and more keep on coming...well, that's a battle.

No one said a word as the grisly old warrior turned and walked out into the Vietnamese night.

Chapter Thirty-Five

On 14 April Tango 1-1 drew an overnight recon patrol. I told my team not to pack any food because we'd be going in late in the day and would be lifted out the next morning.

The mission would prove uneventful. We moved a few hundred meters after dark and set up in a tree-line to watch a series of intersecting paddy dikes to see if there were enemy troops moving through the area. The next morning, we continued observing the area outside the tree-line until 1000 hours when I called for an extraction. The radio relay team on a nearby fire base reported that there was a major battle going on in another part of the AO and all the Brigade helicopters were supporting the infantry, ferrying in more troops and hauling out the dead and wounded. They told us to 'go to ground' and they would send a helicopter when they could.

Later in the day, there was still no word on our extraction. I began to regret my decision not to bring any food on the mission. We spotted a banana tree 30 yards down the tree-line we were hiding in and plucked a few of the ripe fruit to put something in our stomachs. Just before dark, the relay team called and told us that we wouldn't be able to get out until the next morning. The news only made our stomachs growl even more.

It was 1130 hours the next day when the single Huey showed up and brought us back to Tan An. We headed straight for the mess hall. When we got there at 1230 hours, we discovered that the door was locked and the mess hall was closed. We looked through the screened door and could see that there was still food on line in the steam tables. I knocked on the door and the mess sergeant came up from the back of the dining room and said: 'We're closed. Come back at 1700.' I snapped back: 'I can see the food is still out and we haven't eaten in two days. Let us in.' He snarled: 'I told you we're closed', then turned to walk away. I'd had enough of this. I shouted through the screen door:

CHAPTER THIRTY-FIVE

'IF YOU DON'T OPEN THIS DOOR I'LL TEAR IT OFF ITS HINGES, AND YOU HAD BEST NOT BE IN THE WAY WHEN I DO!' The squatty staff sergeant quickly opened the door and off he went, fast-pedaling toward our orderly room.

My teammates and I went inside, put our weapons on an empty table, filled our trays and sat down to eat. Five minutes later, Lieutenant Zapata came storming in and demanded to know if I had threatened the mess sergeant. I said: 'No, Sir, we just had a difference of opinion', as we continued to eat. He stood there for a minute or so, then blurted out: 'You were supposed to give me a de-briefing.' Without looking up from my meal, I answered: 'I will be there as soon as we finish here.' Without another word, Lieutenant Zapata turned on his heel and stormed back to the orderly room.

When we were done eating, I stopped in to give him my de-briefing and quickly put the confrontation in the back of my mind. I found out later that Lieutenant Zapata had called Captain Dickey at Dong Tam and complained that we had broken into the mess hall and threatened the mess sergeant. However, with Captain Dickey being a gentleman and a scholar and a true leader of men, I never heard another word about the incident.

Chapter Thirty-Six

Two teams from the 9th Division's Ranger Company had been sent far south to Fire Base Danger at the request of the infantry battalion working the area at the southern tip of Vietnam near the South China Sea. The teams had been there for a couple of weeks, living in a culvert inside the compound. They rotated pulling recon missions around the fire base, sometimes being inserted by helicopter and sometimes by truck. First Lieutenant Rocker, one of the Ranger officers, and a two-man radio relay team were also stationed on the fire base. Although Rocker was nominally in charge of the fourteen Rangers, he was having difficulty with the lieutenant colonel in command of the infantry battalion. The senior officer had decided that since the Rangers were op-con (operational control) to his battalion, he would make the decisions how and when the teams would be used.

On 16 April, the colonel decided that he wanted one of the two Ranger teams to carry out a recon patrol a few klicks outside the perimeter. Team 2-9 got the nod. Team 2-9 was led by Staff Sergeant Bruce Nichols, a newly-appointed team leader who had just been promoted to his present rank. His ATL was Sergeant Miles Wooley. Specialist Fourth Class Bob Evans and Corporal Steve Patterson were experienced members of the team. The remaining two Rangers were Private First Class Terry Leishman and Private First Class Ron Wayons; both men had just joined the Rangers and each had only a single patrol under their belt.

The team inserted at last light in an open area 100 meters away from a narrow wood-line. Evans took point with the TL, Nichols, walking his slack. Leishman was in the three-slot with the other new guy, Wayons, behind him. Patterson took the five-slot and the ATL, Wooley, walked 'drag'. On Team 2-9, the TL and ATL humped their own radios.

Their recon zone was farm country and was made up of hundreds of rice paddies, separated by a myriad of dikes. Here and there were narrow tree-lines bordering the irrigation ditches and small canals that crisscrossed the area.

The team moved through the knee-high grass covering the LZ until they reached a narrow tree-line 100 meters away from their LZ. They 'went ghost' among the nipa palms and underbrush for almost an hour, watching and listening to make sure their insertion had not drawn anyone's interest.

Finally, satisfied that they had made it in unnoticed, they moved out across the open terrain alert to anything out of the ordinary. Three hours later, they stopped in another wood-line and rested for twenty minutes, then moved out again and continued patrolling until an hour before daylight. In the open country around Fire Support Base Danger, it was foolhardy to move during the light of day.

The team found a thick but narrow patch of woods and moved into the center of it to set up a circular hide site just before dawn. There were rice paddies in all directions, with similar patches of woods on the far sides of them. Nichols put two Rangers on guard while the other four curled up to catch a few hours of sleep. They planned to spend the entire day hidden in the thick cover, then move out again on patrol after darkness set in.

Just before 1000 hours Patterson and Leishman who had been on guard woke up their replacements and lay back to grab some sleep. Five minutes later, both Rangers were awakened by Nichols. He put a finger to his lips to silence them and then pointed across the open rice paddies to a tree-line 300 meters away. Patterson and Leishman cautiously sat up. They noticed their four teammates were already awake and were staring out to the west. The two men rubbed the sleep from their eyes and looked out to see what they were watching. That's when they saw a column of five Viet Cong walking along a distant paddy dike. They had just come out of a wood-line and were heading right for the hidden Rangers.

Nichols thought they had been spotted, but the enemy soldiers appeared to be walking casually with their weapons slung over their shoulders, chatting among themselves. They were unaware of the team watching them from cover. The Ranger team leader hoped that the VC would turn away before they got too close, but it soon appeared that the five men were heading for the same tree-line where the Rangers knelt in hiding.

Nichols whispered for Wayons to watch their back side and ordered everyone else to get on line facing the oncoming VC. When the enemy soldiers were only 75 ft away, Nichols whispered to shoot the ones in the rear first. With that, the TL opened fire on the approaching VC, with the weapons of his four teammates chiming in simultaneously. Each Ranger fired well-aimed single shots and in seconds, all five enemy soldiers were down. Suddenly, the two VC who had been in the front of the column got back to their feet and sprinted for the wood-line they had just left. Weaving back and forth to throw off the aim of the ambushers, both men succeeded in reaching the safety of the trees.

Nichols could tell that the escaping VC had both been hit in the initial ambush, but he thought it unwise to pursue them across the open terrain. The six Rangers stood up and moved out to check the bodies lying in the rice paddy. They recovered some papers and a few piasters from the fallen soldiers, then picked up a pair of AK-47s and an SKS carbine. One of the VC was wearing an AK-47 magazine vest, while the other two men had only the ammunition that was in their weapons.

Moving back to the cover of the tree-line, Nichols contacted the radio relay team and requested an extraction. He was told to 'wait one' while the operator contacted Lieutenant Rocker. A short time later, he came back on line and said that 'Higher-higher, denied your request. You are to continue mission.'

The Ranger knew instantly that 'Higher-higher' was the battalion commander. He had overridden Lieutenant Rocker's authority and made the decision not to extract the team. Nichols struggled to hide his anger, then told his teammates what was happening. He gathered them together and said: 'It's okay, we'll just walk back in to the fire base and extract ourselves.' They all nodded in affirmation.

The team moved out and crossed several rice paddies before holing up again in a thick patch of palm trees. They remained there the rest of the day. After dark they moved out again, heading in the direction of Fire Support Base Danger. They walked most of the night, stopping only for an occasional break. They moved into another patch of dense cover two hours before daylight and took turns sleeping until 1000 hours.

They moved out again a short time later, alert for any sign of danger. The Rangers did not like moving during the day, but Nichols did not look forward to spending another night in the bush. Just after noon, the point man threw up his hand to stop the patrol. They had just come out of a grassy area and Wooley had spotted a large circular object sitting on an open approach to a paddy dike. He eased up to it and discovered that he was looking at the back side of a 40lb Chicom Claymore mine. There was a charging cord running from the back of the mine, disappearing a few meters into a patch of brushy cover. Wooley stepped up to the back of the Claymore and yanked out the cord, rendering the mine harmless. Quickly, he picked it up and returned to the patrol.

The Rangers took turns carrying the heavy mine and the captured enemy weapons until they reached a patch of palm trees several hundred meters outside the FSB Danger perimeter. Nichols grabbed his radio and called the relay team to tell them to alert the guards that there was a patrol coming in from the south. They waited a few minutes to give the relay team time to get the word out, then broke from the cover and crossed the open terrain to the front gate of the fire base.

It was nearly 1500 hours when the Rangers were safely inside. They hid the Claymore until they reached their culvert. They soon joined the members of the other team to discuss their displeasure at the base commander's lack of understanding of how Rangers worked. Late that night, Nichols pulled the captured Claymore out from under a C-ration box where he had hidden it and slipped out into the night.

The next morning, the infantry battalion commander stepped out of his hooch after a comfortable night of sleep only to stare slack-jawed at the sight of a 40lb Chicom Claymore pointed directly at his doorway with a cord running from the back side out over the concertina wire on the perimeter of the base camp. Shortly after this incident, Lieutenant Rocker took the two Ranger teams and the radio relay personnel back to Dong Tam. No one ever learned how the VC had managed to plant the Chicom mine in front of the battalion commander's quarters, or why they had run 100ft of parachute cord from the back of it out to the perimeter wire. Some things are just destined to remain a mystery.

Chapter Thirty-Seven

On 17 April Tango 1-1 moved back to Dong Tam. We would be there for about three weeks running missions. I had just been assigned my first patrol and was getting my gear ready when Sergeant First Class Ray Sonnier approached me and asked if I wanted to use his raincoat. As it was raining lightly at the time, I smiled at him and said: 'Sure. Thanks.'

The brief mission was uneventful and when we arrived back at Dong Tam I went to his hooch and placed the folded raincoat on his bunk. Unknown to either myself or Sergeant First Class Sonnier, one of the company's junior officers came by a short time later, saw the raincoat on the bunk and, since it was still raining, decided to 'borrow' it.

After I had left Sonnier's hooch, I had gone to take a shower to wash away the mud and grime from the mission. After finishing, I put on a pair of shorts and flip-flops and joined a couple of other Rangers in the club to enjoy a cold beer and shoot some pool. I was leaning across the pool table about ready to bank the 9-ball into a corner pocket when Sonnier entered the club and bellowed: 'THAYER, WHERE IN THE F**K IS MY RAINCOAT?' Then he followed it up with a boot to my backside.

Without thinking, I turned and slugged him in the forehead right between his eyes. He collapsed to the floor like he had been pole-axed and lay there unmoving. I stood there, rubbing my knuckles, waiting for him to come around, still mad as hell about the kick to my posterior, and not giving a thought about the repercussions of striking a superior. Sergeant Mike Calog and another Ranger finally picked up the slowly recovering senior NCO and walked him back to his hooch. Mike returned a short time later and announced: 'Well, Jim, there goes a stripe.' He laughed and slapped me on the back. For some reason, I didn't see the humor in his statement.

An hour later, I put my cue stick in the rack and returned to my room to get some sleep. I was walking across the compound when I saw

Captain Dickey approaching. I thought to myself that I was about to get a severe tongue-lashing, followed by the announcement that I was no longer a staff sergeant, but as he passed me he just shook his head and continued walking. I never heard another word about the incident. I found out years later that Captain Dickey had 'handled' the matter by giving Sergeant First Class Sonnier an in-country R&R to Vung Tau to get him out of the unit until the matter cooled down. I returned to Tan An not long after and never ran into Sonnier again while I was in Vietnam.

Chapter Thirty-Eight

It was on the morning of 25 May that I received word that Captain Dickey wanted to see me down in Dong Tam. I made the arrangements to bum a ride with a three-quarter-ton truck making a mail run to the Division base camp and left Tan An around noon.

When I arrived at the Ranger Headquarters, I reported in to my Commanding Officer and was told to take a seat. Captain Dickey dispensed with the small talk and showed me a sealed registered letter from a law firm back in the States. He seemed worried, but I laughed and said: 'I know what it is. Please, Cap, open it.'

Dickey sat back in his chair and pulled a letter-opener out of a drawer in the center of his desk. He opened one end of the letter and removed its contents. After reading the cover page, he affirmed my initial thoughts. 'It's divorce papers from a law firm representing your wife.' I nodded and told him: 'I'd been expecting this, Sir.'

Captain Dickey looked up from the letter, hesitated a moment, then offered: 'Sergeant Thayer, I'm going to send you back to the States to see if you can work things out.' Shrugging my shoulders, I said: 'Thanks, but I'm not sure that will do any good.' He peered at me intently and added: 'Well go and try anyway. I don't want this hanging over your head while you're fighting a war halfway around the world.'

Sensing that the meeting was over, I stood and saluted him, then turned and left his office. I stopped by the company clerk who made me wait while he typed up my leave paperwork and handed me copies of my personnel file.

I went back to my barracks to pack my civilian clothes for the trip back to California, then caught a ride to Tan Son Nhut for the long flight home. I had little hope that my marriage was salvageable, but if Captain Dickey was willing to give me the opportunity to find out, I would make the best of the effort.

CHAPTER THIRTY-EIGHT

I arrived at Travis Air Force Base the next day and took a military shuttle to the Oakland Army Depot. After clearing Customs, I bought tickets for a bus ride to my home two hours away. It was nearly 1930 hours when I stepped out of a taxi and walked up to my door and knocked. She opened it, showed a little surprise, then said: 'What are you doing here?' I looked at her and replied: 'I guess I'm here to see if we could patch things up.' Still holding on to the door, she sneered: 'No. You need to leave.'

My baby daughter began crying in the room behind her, so I brushed past my wife and went over to pick her up. When she finally stopped crying, I turned back to my wife and asked: 'Where is my dog?' Still standing at the open door, she said: 'I got rid of him, your clothes and all your personal property. You have nothing left here. So just get out.' I could see that she was growing angrier by the minute, but I wasn't about to back down yet. 'What about the flight jacket my brother, Mel, gave me?' I demanded. 'I gave it to my boyfriend. Now if you don't go, I'll call the police.' The hatred in her eyes told me that she was dead serious, but I was in too deep to back down now. I snapped at her: 'You go right ahead and call them.' I watched her cross the room, pick up the telephone and call the local police precinct to file a complaint.

It wasn't long before two uniformed officers and a detective showed up at the door of the apartment. The detective stepped inside when my wife opened the door and said: 'What's going on here?' She pointed at me and told him: 'I want him out of the house. I filed for a divorce and I don't want him here.'

The detective turned to me. Before he said a thing, he looked down at the Silver Star ribbon on my uniform. He asked me about it, so I handed him my personnel folder and leave orders. He took the time to look through the paperwork in my folder, then turned back to my wife and said: 'Lady, you should be ashamed of yourself. He has as much of a right here as you do.' Flabbergasted, her voice broke when she muttered: 'Well, if he is staying, I'm going.' I interrupted her, and offered: 'Not a problem, you stay. I'm going to San Francisco.'

The detective put his hand on my shoulder and told me that he would be honored to drive me to the bus station. I kissed my daughter goodbye and handed her back to my wife, looked at them both for the final time, then walked out to the police car behind the detective.

I spent the next few days in San Francisco. I knew a bartender at a bar I used to occasionally drink at when I had been stationed at the Presidio during my first enlistment. He was kind enough to listen to my sorrowful tale, then introduce me to a young lady he was friends with. We spent the rest of my leave together until it was time for me to return to the war.

Before I left San Francisco, I decided that I needed to buy a handgun to take back to Vietnam with me. I found a gun store and purchased a .45 caliber long Colt revolver. I also picked up a leather gun belt and clamshell holster with a button in the finger hole that when pressed would pop the revolver up out of the holster. I planned to wear the rig under my shirt during my return to the war.

I did a lot of soul-searching on the long flight back to Vietnam. My marriage had been a disaster, and I found several things for which both of us were at fault. I couldn't put all the blame on my wife. I decided that, in the long run, it was probably best for both of us that it had ended, but the loss of my baby girl would plague me for the rest of my life.

When I got back to my company at Dong Tam, I reported directly to Captain Dickey and told him that things hadn't worked out. I thanked him for giving me the opportunity to attempt a reconciliation, but I had accepted the fact that the divorce was best for both of us. He shook my hand and told me that he was sorry about my situation and asked me if I was ready to get back into the fight. When I nodded, he told me that he was sending me back to my team in Tan An. Having burned my bridges behind me, I was indeed ready to return to the war.

Chapter Thirty-Nine

I arrived back at Tan An on 31 May only to discover that a tragedy had befallen my team during my absence. After my departure to the States, Lieutenant Zapata had decided that he couldn't afford to have a team on stand-down until I got back to Vietnam. He assigned a newly-arrived staff sergeant by the name of Curtis Daniels to serve as the team leader for Tango 1-1 until I returned. I had met Daniels just before I had left. He seemed like a great guy and we had become fast friends. He had just transferred into the unit from a line company and had served an earlier tour with the 1st Brigade of the 101st Airborne Division. Unfortunately, he had no experience as an LRP/Ranger team leader. Our unit had always required that inexperienced newcomers go out on a few missions as the low man on the team before being assigned positions of leadership responsibility. For some unknown reason, Lieutenant Zapata had violated that rule and had given Daniels the team leader position on Tango 1-1 right after I left. It was a mistake that had proved fatal.

The team had gone out on a recon mission and had entered a village to check for enemy troops that had been spotted in the area. Daniels had asked an elderly Vietnamese civilian they were questioning where the VC were hiding. The old man pointed to a spot outside the village indicating the VC were there. For reasons not known, Staff Sergeant Daniels split the five-man team into two elements, taking Volheim and Mike Kentes with him to go check out the spot where the old man had pointed. The other two Rangers, Christiansen and Valenti, remained behind with the old man.

When the three men reached the wooded area the elderly Vietnamese had identified, several VC hidden in the nearby trees opened fire from close range, killing Daniels and Volheim outright and wounding Kentes. Kentes was smart enough to play dead while the Viet Cong stepped out of the cover and checked the bodies. Kentes didn't move when one of the VC poked a weapon in his back, then knelt to remove his web gear.

Back at the village, Christiansen and Valenti had heard the firing and came running toward the ambush site. The enemy soldiers saw them coming and fled back into the trees. The two men quickly reached the spot where their comrades lay. They checked the bodies of the two dead Rangers. Seeing that Kentes was still alive, Christiansen dressed his wounds while Valenti stood guard. When Christiansen had finished treating his wounded teammate, he called for a medevac helicopter and a slick to extract the remainder of the team. The mission had been a total disaster.

I was angry when I heard what had happened to my team during my absence. At first I blamed myself for not being there, but I soon reasoned that it was the ill-advised decision to put an inexperienced man in my place that had caused the deaths of two good Rangers and the wounding of a third. I made up my mind then and there that I would never allow myself to lose a man because of a stupid mistake or an error in judgment. Life was too dear and too fragile to end it through the folly of a misguided decision.

Chapter Forty

The day after my return to Tan An, Lieutenant Zapata approached me and said: 'Sergeant, how would you like to go with me and take a couple of teams into that village where Daniels and Volheim were killed to check it for VC?' I looked him in the eyes and replied: 'Yes, Sir, let's do it.' I wanted to tell him that the deaths of Daniels and Volheim were on his shoulders, but I thought better of it at the time.

Zapata quickly put a couple of teams together, the bulk of them made up of new arrivals in the company. It was risky taking untested soldiers on this type of mission, so I decided that I would do my best to look out for them during the patrol.

I gathered the two teams together and went over my plan for the coming operation. We would go in 'light', inserted by a pair of US Navy patrol boats. After we made it ashore, the boats would pull out and move a short distance away to a secure location in a canal to wait for a call from us for extraction. I told them that I didn't believe the mission would last more than a few hours.

At first, everything seemed to go according to plan. The patrol boats dropped us off on the shoreline and quickly withdrew to a nearby canal to await our signal. We paused long enough for the sound of the boats to die out, then broke cover and began our patrol toward the hamlet. It didn't take us long before we were set up in a hide site monitoring the activity in and around the village. Observing the area for nearly thirty minutes and seeing no enemy soldiers, we entered the village, split into two separate elements and began searching each of the hooches and the bunkers inside them. We were looking for VC, weapons and contraband.

We soon discovered a pair of Vietnamese women standing in a hut near the center of the village. One of the women was elderly, but the other appeared to be around 25 to 30 years old and was dressed in black pajamas. She was very attractive and looked to be of French/Vietnamese descent. While we were searching the hut, I couldn't help but notice that while the elderly woman remained stoic and detached, the younger woman glared at us with such an obvious contempt that it sent chills up my spine. She watched every move we made, and if looks could kill we would have all been pushing up daisies. I had one of my PRUs question her, asking her if she was VC, but she vehemently denied that she was, nor would she admit to knowing anything about them. I was certain she was lying, but since I had no real proof, I decided to leave her with the old woman and get on with the search.

After checking nearly all the structures in the village, we moved toward the final one, intent on getting it over with before returning to the river for extraction. It was at that moment that we spotted a pair of armed Viet Cong running along a paddy dike outside the village, then disappearing into a large bunker on the edge of a wood-line less than 100 meters away. It happened so quickly, no one had a chance to fire them up.

I called both teams together and told them to take cover behind the hooch. Lieutenant Zapata and I discussed what action we should take, then decided that the best thing to do would be to fire a couple of LAWs (Light Anti-Tank Weapons) into the bunker. Two of the Rangers knelt at the edge of the village, prepared the LAWs to fire, then launched the deadly rockets into the front wall of the bunker. Both rounds were on the money. After the smoke had cleared and the dust had settled, we could see that the rockets had caused little physical damage to the bunker. Realizing that we had no ordnance with us strong enough to knock out the earthen/log structure and unwilling to assault it across 100 meters of open ground, I suggested to Lieutenant Zapata that we might want to call in an airstrike to handle the situation. He readily agreed and was soon busy on the radio calling for support from the Air Force.

I took a seat on a crude wooden chair in front of the hooch to watch the coming air show. An elderly man who lived in the structure came outside and stood behind me. When the two F-4s arrived on-station, several other Rangers moved up to my left and right to get a good view of the bomb runs.

Lieutenant Zapata radioed the location of the bunker to the pilots, describing exactly where it was situated on the edge of the wood-line. The fighter-bombers dropped out of the sky several hundred meters apart and made their bomb runs coming in from our right side.

Each plane dropped a 250lb bomb directly on the large bunker. It was indeed a beautiful thing to behold. The ground shook visibly from the nearby impact of the bombs. As the smoke was clearing, we could see that there was nothing left of the bunker but a large crater where it had previously stood. No one inside could have survived such a blast. As a rousing cheer broke out from the gathered Rangers in appreciation of the Air Force's impressive accuracy, a red-hot jagged chunk of metal nearly 3in long came whizzing in to plop on the ground right between my bare feet. I looked down at the still-smoking metal shard and thought to myself: 'Wow, now that was really cool!'

When I turned around to comment to my teammates who had been standing on either side of me, I soon discovered that I was suddenly alone. Even the elderly Vietnamese man who had been standing right behind me was nowhere to be seen. Looking around, I laughed and shouted: 'Hey, where did you all go? This thing's not going to chase you down.'

I got up from the chair and went to locate Lieutenant Zapata. When I found him, he had just finished giving the Air Force pilots a brief-back on the success of their air strike. When he signed off, I told him that there was nothing else we could do here. He agreed and radioed for the patrol boats to meet us back at the shoreline for an extraction in twenty minutes. We would never know for certain if we killed the same VC who had ambushed Tango 1-1, but it was nice to believe we had gotten a little payback.

We left the village, moving out in patrol formation. When we reached the river a short time later, the patrol boats were there waiting for us, standing just offshore. When the crew saw us break out of the cover and move down to the water's edge, they roared in to recover both teams for the short trip back to Tan An.

Chapter Forty-One

I was glad to have the last patrol behind me. I wanted to forget about the two guys who had been killed while I was wasting my time in California trying to salvage a marriage that I had known was over. It was time to rebuild my team and get on with my job. I still had Sef Gallardo, Chris Valenti and Mike Kentes, plus Bao and Dien. Bill Christiansen had also gone out with the team on occasion and was there with Chris Valenti when Daniels and Volheim had been killed and Kentes wounded. There were also a couple of new guys who had just arrived in Tan An that needed to be broken in, but most of the time I would continue running missions with my mainstays: Gallardo, Valenti, Kentes, Bao and Dien.

During the months of May and June my team had run a lot of unsuccessful Parakeet flights with no contact to show for the effort. The Parakeet flights consisted of flying around at altitude in a Huey slick while an LOH scout helicopter flew low-level trying to locate and flush small bands of VC out into the open. Once the enemy had been spotted, the Huey would then spiral down to drop off the small Ranger killer teams to engage and wipe out the fleeing enemy soldiers. This type of operation had racked up some heavy enemy body counts for our unit over the past several months but had also proven costly in wounded and dead Rangers.

Tango 1-1 ran fifteen to twenty Parakeet operations during the two-month period, but not once were we able to locate the enemy. Either the VC had gotten wise to our Parakeet flights or we had encountered an extended streak of very bad luck.

I was anxious to get back to the normal ground patrols that seemed to improve our odds of success. I had nothing against the Parakeet flights, but they would never replace the satisfaction of sneaking in and catching the enemy by surprise.

Chapter Forty-Two

On 6 June Lieutenant Zapata ordered me to get my team ready for an overnight patrol to recon an area through which concentrations of enemy troops had been observed moving during the hours of darkness. He informed us that the entire AO was considered a 'free-fire zone', which meant that we could blow away anyone we encountered. There were no rules of engagement and no friendlies there to worry about.

I returned to the barracks to gather up my teammates. I walked into the open bay and shouted: 'Let's go, Tango 1-1. We've got a mission. Moving out in ten mikes [minutes].' We grabbed our weapons and gear, applied a quick coat of camo face paint, and headed out for the helipad. As I usually did, I climbed into the chopper and moved up between the pilot and co-pilot to show them the spot on my map I had chosen for an LZ. They marked the spot on their own maps, then gave me a thumbs-up to indicate they were good to go.

The Huey dropped us in a large clearing of knee-high kunai grass and short reeds. Since there was little concealment in the LZ, we sprinted to a nearby palm/banana grove that offered heavy ground cover beneath the trees. While we 'played ghost', I checked my map and determined that we were almost 300 meters from the trail I had planned to monitor.

We moved out in patrol formation with Bao at point and me at 'slack'. Valenti was behind me with the radio, followed by Kentes, Gallardo (my ATL), and Dien pulling rear security. We moved slowly, watching for booby-traps or any other signs of the enemy.

When we finally reached the heavily-used trail, we moved into a defensive position close enough for us to observe foot traffic up and down the high-speed trail, yet far enough back in the deep cover that we would not be seen or heard by anyone passing by on it. Just before 1630 hours, we spotted a middle-aged Vietnamese man, a woman and a child pass by on the trail. They never gave any indication that they were aware we were there watching them.

At 1900 hours it was totally dark and we could no longer visually monitor the trail through the dense underbrush. I whispered to my teammates that I wanted to move out across a nearby rice paddy and set up a new OP where we could observe the trail where it left the cover and crossed the open paddy. In addition, my map indicated there was a small village not far from the spot I had selected, so we would be in position to keep our eyes on it as well.

We slipped out of the brush and moved silently across the open field to a point where two paddy dikes met. Some low vegetation grew along the back side of the dikes, providing just enough concealment to break up our silhouettes. When we reached the spot, I had each of my teammates set up within reach of the man next to him, so that he would be able to wake him during the night to stand watch when his turn came. We had brought along a Starlight scope, and the quarter-moon slowly sliding across the heavens would provide plenty of ambient light to enable us to observe anyone moving out on the trail where it crossed the open rice paddy.

There was water in the paddy at the base of the dike we hid behind. Since I was barefoot, I decided to slip my feet into the shallow water to keep the mosquitoes from feasting on my exposed skin. I had already taped my pants tight against my lower legs with electrical tape to keep the leeches from using them as a highway to my family jewels.

We remained in place the remainder of the night. Just before dawn, we slipped back across the rice paddy to a more concealed spot inside the underbrush where we could still observe traffic out on the trail. Once we were set up, I radioed our relay team to report negative sightings and negative contact. I then requested an update on our orders. They came back minutes later and told us to move to the west to monitor an area where the high-speed trail exited the small hamlet and meandered out into the open countryside. They added that we would be notified of our extraction later in the day.

Bao whispered to me that he was hungry and suggested that we find something to eat. Reluctantly, I told him to go and see what he could come up with. Thirty minutes later, he came back and reported that he had spotted a single hooch not far away from our position. I moved the patrol out, sticking to the denser cover until I sighted the hooch just up ahead.

We moved in slowly, until we had the small hut surrounded. It proved to be a two-room structure occupied by an older Vietnamese man and his wife. The hut sat on a small piece of ground a foot or two higher than the jungle that bordered it on three sides and a small rice paddy about 15 meters to the front. Off to one side, chickens were feeding in a small pen surrounding a tiny hutch. Bao suggested that he would ask them if they would make us some chicken and rice. I told him to have at it.

I watched as he approached the old man and engaged in a rather prolonged conversation. The old fellow seemed unwilling to cooperate at first, but finally agreed to prepare a meal for us. I saw him smile and nod in the affirmative after Bao finished talking to him. The old couple quickly dispatched one of the birds, plucked it, chopped it into pieces and dropped it in a large cooking pot. We sat around the front of the hut, keeping an eye on the far side of the rice paddy while the meat was cooking. After it was ready, the elderly couple served us rice on banana leaves with the steaming chicken pieces ladled over the top. The food was quite tasty but then, it could have been that we were just very hungry. We rested for thirty minutes after we finished eating. While we were sitting back relaxing, Bao whispered to me that he had to promise the old man that we would pay him for the meal. Now I knew why the old man had changed his mind. I gave Bao some MPC (Military Payment Currency) and told him to give it to the elderly couple and express our deep gratitude for their generous hospitality. Their eyes lit up when Bao handed them the valuable bills. It was only 10 dollars in American money, but to them it was probably more money than they saw in a month.

Before we had sat down to eat, I had placed Dien in a spot where he could observe our backtrail while he ate his meal. Just as I was preparing to get the patrol up and moving again, Dien came running up to where the remainder of the team was located and told us that there were people approaching from the south. We hurriedly gathered up our weapons, thanked the elderly Vietnamese couple again and moved off quickly to the north. Around 100 meters away from the hooch, we slipped into some heavy cover to observe the area we had just left. We waited for several minutes, and when no one showed up at the hut, I decided that it was a good time to take some evasive actions just in case we had company coming after us. We moved another 300 meters in a different direction before finally arriving at the village that the trail ran through.

We found a great spot, well-hidden back in the brush, to set up an OP to monitor the village.

A few hours later, I called in a sitrep (situation report) and was told to move to our PZ (Pick-up Zone) for extraction. The PZ that had been selected was only 200 meters away from our present location. I was certain that the decision to pull us out before dark was due to the fact that we hadn't brought any rations with us. Lieutenant Zapata must have figured that we would likely be getting pretty hungry by the end of the second day, so he thought he was doing us a favor by extracting the team a few hours early.

We backed away from our OP and moved quietly to the edge of a small open area between a couple of expansive rice paddies. When the lift ship radioed that it was five mikes out from our location, we popped a yellow smoke grenade and tossed it out into the clearing. Two minutes later, a voice crackled on the radio: 'Tango 1-1, this is Ghost-Rider 2-3, I copy yellow smoke, over.' I answered back: 'Roger yellow smoke. Good to go, Ghost-Rider 2-3. Tango 1-1, out.'

Then the Huey was on the ground in the middle of the PZ. We mounted up quickly for the short flight back to Tan An. Like most of our missions, it had been interesting but had proven uneventful.

When we landed at Tan An, I sent the team off to the showers and went to debrief Lieutenant Zapata. I chose to omit the part of the mission about dining out with the Vietnamese family. I figured that it was better to let him think he had done us a big favor by pulling us out early.

Chapter Forty-Three

On the night of 11 June, Lieutenant Zapata spent the evening drinking at the Officers' Club with a Navy SEAL officer. Both men began swapping war stories about the successes of their relative units. Before the night had ended, Lieutenant Zapata had issued an invitation for the SEAL lieutenant to accompany one of his Ranger teams on a Parakeet flight.

The next morning the lieutenant approached Staff Sergeant Jimmy Booth and told him that he wanted the NCO to fly C&C (Command and Control) on a Parakeet flight. He mentioned that a Navy SEAL lieutenant would be accompanying the team, then added: 'Sergeant Booth, I want you to make sure we get some action for this SEAL officer.' Booth replied: 'I understand, Lieutenant. Can do.'

Zapata then sought me out and asked me if I'd like to go out on a mission. I asked: 'What have you got, Sir?' He repeated the story he had related to Booth, stressing that it was really important to him to show this SEAL lieutenant just how Rangers operated in the field. After listening to what Lieutenant Zapata had to say, I must admit that I was a little miffed. Zapata had obviously let his mouth overload his brain, and now he was asking me and my teammates to put on a show for this squid lieutenant. The only bad thing about it was that we were risking our lives just to make him look good. Well, we risked our lives every time we went out to the field, so I guess it didn't make that much difference. I replied: 'Why not, Sir. Sounds like fun. How many guys do you want?'

He seemed relieved that I had accepted his challenge and offered: 'Just you and three others. The SEAL lieutenant and I and my RTO will make it a seven-man team.' I nodded, and went to round up Gallardo, Valenti and Kentes. I told them to pack 'light'. It was a Parakeet mission and we'd only be out for a few hours. Gallardo carried an M79 with forty rounds of HE (high-explosive) grenades. I carried my modified CAR-15 and wore a sleeveless camo vest, open in the front. The two officers each carried CAR-15s, while the rest of my teammates and the RTO brought standard M16s. I also decided that this would be a good time to go barefoot, figuring that ought to REALLY serve to impress this SEAL officer. With my headband, I looked more like a Mandalay pirate than a US Army Ranger.

It was not uncommon in E Company (Ranger) for an officer to go out on patrol. When they did, they seldom played the role of team leader, but on this mission Lieutenant Zapata decided to do just that. Since nearly half the team consisted of personnel not part of Tango 1-1, I didn't mind relinquishing my role as team leader.

A short time later, Staff Sergeant Booth returned to the team barracks and announced that everything was a 'go' for the Parakeet flight. The aviation assets had been laid on and the Huey was already waiting for us on the helipad. An LOH scout helicopter armed with a mini-gun would link up with us as soon as we were airborne. Satisfied that everything was ready, my three teammates and I accompanied Booth to the waiting Huey slick.

The two officers and their RTO met us at the helipad. Lieutenant Zapata greeted us, looked us over like it was something he always did, then said: 'Okay, men, if everyone's ready, let's take off.' We crowded aboard the Huey and took up our normal positions on the aircraft floor. We couldn't help but notice that Lieutenant Zapata and the Navy SEAL sat on the fold-down seats located against the rear firewall. As we lifted away from the helipad, the pilot of the LOH radioed the aircraft commander of the Huey and told him that he was having engine problems and would catch up with the Huey after he returned to base to have it checked out.

We headed west toward the Cambodian border. I was sitting in my usual spot on the cabin floor next to the port-side door gunner with my legs dangling outside the aircraft when a strange sensation suddenly came over me. I was smoking a cigarette, cupping it in my hand against the wind, when a voice whispered in my ear: 'You're going to get shot in the chest.'

Maybe it wasn't a voice I heard. Maybe it was just my imagination. All that I can say is that I had a very strong premonition at that moment that I was going to catch a bullet in my vitals. It was enough to cause me some extreme momentary anxiety. It was the second time during my tour that I had an experience that could only be described as spiritual or supernatural. Whatever it was, I found it very unsettling. Finding that my cigarette suddenly tasted bitter, I tossed it out into the slipstream, slid back inside the chopper and began pondering the mysterious warning I had just received.

Ten minutes had passed when I felt the pitch of the turbine change as the aircraft dropped rapidly toward the ground. The Huey pilot had just spotted several VC near a pair of hooches several hundred meters away. One of the structures appeared to have a thatched roof, while the other one was larger with a red tiled roof.

I slid back into position on the edge of the cabin floor, my feet just above the skids as the aircraft banked sharply, coming around to the left. It flared to a gut-wrenching hover above an old rice paddy located just behind the two buildings. While still aboard the aircraft, I spotted several VC rushing around the sides of the hooches and disappearing inside. One of them turned and leaned out the door to see what we were going to do. The port-side door gunner and I opened fire on him as my teammates and I dropped to the ground and began running toward the structures. The rice paddy was muddy, which cushioned our landing but also hampered our forward movement.

The two officers and their radioman ran to the right and took cover behind a 2ft-high lip of elevated ground that supported the two buildings. Valenti and Kentes sprinted to the left and dove behind the high ground on the opposite side of the hooches. Gallardo and I charged right up the middle. Suddenly, the VC began pouring out of both structures, attempting to escape into the tree-line to the rear. I stopped in the muddy field to take some of them out with quick well-aimed single shots. Gallardo asked me where he should fire his M79 and I shouted for him to start dropping rounds ahead of a group of Viet Cong running for the woods behind the buildings. He fired several rounds in the general direction, then turned his weapon toward the hooches and began placing HE rounds up close and personal.

Off to the left, Valenti and Kentes were also firing at the fleeing VC. They hit one enemy soldier who ran from the larger hooch with an arm full of rifles. Struck high in the back, the VC went down hard with the weapons flying everywhere. I couldn't believe that there were that many VC bailing out of the buildings. It reminded me of angry hornets pouring out of a disturbed nest.

As I was trying to take in all the action going down in front of me, another VC, armed with an AK-47, ran out of the hooch nearest to me.

I shot him, but as he was spun around from the impact of my bullet, he managed to squeeze off a short burst that tore up the ground directly in my path. One of his rounds ricocheted and slammed hard into my upper chest.

I had been so busy fighting the VC that I had totally forgotten about the premonition I had on the flight out. Now it came back screaming at me with a vengeance all too real. I had just reached the high ground in front of the huts when I was hit. The force of the round drove me down on my back into the muddy rice paddy. I began digging frantically at my chest, trying to claw out the bullet that had just put me there.

Blood was spurting from the wound in intermittent gushes, which instantly made me think that I was going to bleed out, but a few seconds later, the bleeding slowed to a trickle. Gallardo dropped to a knee in the mud next to me and anxiously pressed his flop hat over the wound as if it would somehow stop the bleeding. I yelled at him to get that dirty damned thing off me and get out a proper field dressing, which he quickly managed to do. I coughed and spit into my hand to see if there was any blood in my sputum. Fortunately for me it was clear. I thought to myself: 'Okay, it's not as bad as I figured.'

I turned to Gallardo and said: 'Hand me my CAR.' Armed again, I struggled out of the mud and got back to my feet. Feeling no pain, I once again charged toward the enemy, firing my weapon as I ran. Gallardo was right on my hip.

Unknown to me at the time, Lieutenant Zapata had witnessed my wounding and had immediately radioed Booth, flying C&C in the Huey. He reported that I had just sustained a sucking chest wound and ordered Booth to call for a medevac. Instead, Booth shouted into his intercom mic at the pilot: 'Hey, there's no way we're leaving Jim Thayer down there wounded until a medevac shows up! Turn this damn thing around.' When the pilot hesitated, Booth snarled: 'I'm not waiting for the medevac. Let's go now.'

The aircraft commander banked the Huey around and flew back to the scene of the firefight. As it flared to a landing near the hooches, Booth saw that I was up on my feet, still fighting with my CAR-15 in my right hand and holding a field dressing to my chest wound with my left.

Suddenly, I heard Lieutenant Zapata shouting: 'MOUNT UP, MOUNT UP! LET'S GO!' I thought to myself: 'What the hell! Why are we leaving? There are bad guys everywhere and weapons laying all over the place.' The look I gave Zapata must have made it pretty clear that I was not happy with his decision to get out of Dodge in the middle of a battle…a battle that we were winning, but being wounded, I didn't think it wise to stay and fight when everyone else was running for the chopper. Reluctantly, I turned to follow Gallardo to the waiting Huey and climbed aboard.

As the aircraft went light on its skids and lifted out of the clearing, I began to feel a little weak. I lay back on the floor of the cabin and the pain that hit me was both instantaneous and unbearable. It felt as if someone was shoving a red-hot poker into my back. When I struggled to sit up again, a couple of my teammates pushed me back down and held me there, believing that sitting up would only cause me to start bleeding again.

Suddenly, I realized what was causing the pain. When I had climbed aboard the chopper, I had tossed my weapon in ahead of me. Now I was laying across the red-hot barrel of my CAR-15. I shouted at the top of my lungs: 'GET MY GUN OUT FROM UNDER ME! IT'S BURNING ME.' Mercifully, one of my teammates understood what was happening and slipped his hand under my back to yank out the still-smoking weapon.

On the way back to Tan An, I was still mad as hell that Lieutenant Zapata had pulled us out of the battle. However, several days later I would realize that he had only been thinking about my welfare when he called for a 'dust-off' and then again when he made the decision to extract the team. His only desire was to get me to a med station as quickly as possible. It was the same with my friend, Jimmy Booth, who had decided that there was no way he was going to leave Thayer on the ground with a sucking chest wound waiting for a medevac chopper to arrive on the scene. I had to admit that it was comforting to know that I had people who had my 'six' (back). That kind of knowledge meant a lot to a man engaged in a battle.

Chapter Forty-Four

When we arrived at the Med Station at Dong Tam, the medics were waiting to help me off the chopper. They put me on a gurney and immediately wheeled me into triage. A technician hurriedly took a couple of X-rays of my chest, then wheeled me into a large well-lit operating room. The room was filled with wounded guys from an infantry unit that had been in a tough battle earlier that morning. There was no place for me, so a doctor moved some items from a work table and the medics slid me onto it. The doctor then climbed up on the table and straddled my mid-section. He gave me a local injection of some type of anesthetic, then cut a slit in my chest about 3in long to expose the path of the round and to give him more room to work. As he was busy doing all of this, he kept explaining the reason for each action. Finally, he started digging and probing into my sternum. The pressure of him pushing down as he cut away tissue and cartilage was a bit painful, and for a moment it felt like he must be working his way through to my back.

The surgeon finally located and removed part of the bullet. Holding it up so that I could see the result of his mining expedition, he announced: 'I got most of it, but there's a small piece lodged against the back side of your sternum. I don't think it will bother you, so I'm just going to leave it there. If you want to, you can have it removed in the future.' I don't recall him waiting for an answer, nor do I remember giving him one. He quickly administered another injection and I was out cold.

I woke up early the next morning. One of those large classroom clocks mounted on the wall indicated that it was almost 0800 hours. I looked around drowsily trying to get my senses back on track and noticed that there was an IV running down to my left arm. When I saw that there was 6in of air in the middle of the tube, I screamed for a medic. He showed up a few seconds later and asked what I needed. I told him to get that IV out of my arm because I didn't want air pumped into me. I was acutely

140

aware of what an embolism could do to one's health. He said: 'Don't worry, Sarge. You see that VC next to you? We've been pumping air into him for hours and he's still here.'

I looked up at him and snarled: 'You think that's funny? Take it out or I'll do it myself.' Convinced that I wasn't joking, he said: 'Hang on for a minute,' then he turned away and summoned a captain who was standing nearby reading a patient's chart. The captain arrived at my bedside and enquired as to what the problem was. I told him that I wanted the IV taken out of my arm and I needed a land line to call my unit. The officer nodded, then told the medic to remove the IV. A short time later, another doctor arrived and stitched up my wound. He dressed it and told me to use peroxide to keep it clean and free of infection.

After he left, the medic brought me a telephone. I called my Company and told them I needed a ride back to the unit. The clerk said he would contact Captain Dickey and get it done. A short time later, a jeep arrived at the med station and took me back to Dong Tam.

When I got to my room, I cleaned and dressed the wound again and went to bed. The next morning when I awoke, I remembered that I was back in the company area. In spite of my pain, it still managed to put a smile on my face. I had never been a fan of laying around in a hospital bed waiting for my body to heal. I found it depressing. Attitude made a big difference when you were trying to regain your health, and my attitude had improved 100 percent when the jeep driver had dropped me off in front of my unit's orderly room. The doctor at the med station had instructed me to come back in a couple of weeks so he could check my progress and remove the wire sutures he had used to close the wound. He had also cautioned me to have the company medic check it daily to change the dressing and make sure there was no infection starting up.

Chapter Forty-Five

On 13 June, the day after I was wounded, Sergeant Mike Calog's team went out on an overnight recon mission in an AO 15 klicks out from Dong Tam. G-2 had just received agent reports of a large NVA unit operating somewhere in the area.

Calog and I had become good friends when I had spent some time at Dong Tam on my return from Japan. He had become a very capable and experienced team leader. The rest of Calog's team consisted of Dennis Lastine as assistant team leader, Norman Crabb, Bob Martin, Billy Clark and their PRU, Nhan, at point. Calog and Lastine carried their own radios on patrol.

The team inserted by helicopter at last light that evening. The cloud cover was sagging lower as the slick dropped them into a small clearing. In the fading daylight, the team moved 50 meters to an old earthen berm with a few bushes growing along the side facing their LZ. Calog signaled his teammates to set up along the back side of the berm for the night. Just across the berm to their front stood a single bamboo hut with a thatched roof. It had been erected on a small, elevated patch of ground overlooking a long rice paddy that extended nearly 100 meters to the north, before ending against a long paddy dike. On the other side of the dike, a large field of kunai grass ran another 200 meters to a large forested area.

The Rangers could see an open doorway on the back side of the hut facing them and could make out another open doorway on the opposite side of the hut facing the rice paddy. There was no light in the structure, which made them believe that it was unoccupied.

Minutes after the team had set up their night defense position behind the berm, the sky closed in on them and a heavy thunderstorm broke out. The Rangers huddled in the driving rain, praying that the downpour would not last long.

CHAPTER FORTY-FIVE

A short time later, the Rangers spotted several tiny points of light spread out through the tree-line 300 meters away on the far side of the hut. The lights appeared stationary. Unable to determine whether they were camp fires, lanterns or flashlights, the Rangers kept their eyes on them.

After an hour had passed, the team leader attempted to call in a scheduled sitrep to the radio relay team operating on a nearby fire support base. He wanted to report the lights that were still visible in the tree-line. After several unsuccessful attempts at reaching the relay team, Calog determined that his radio was not working. Lastine tried to make a connection with his own PRC-25, but quickly discovered that his radio wasn't functioning either. The two Rangers concluded that the rain was the source of their commo problems and decided to move the team into the nearby hooch to try to dry out their radios.

When they reached the back door of the small hut they stepped quickly inside, only to discover that it was indeed occupied by a middle-aged Vietnamese farmer and his wife. They were lying in their bed and appeared very frightened when the six soaking wet camouflaged soldiers entered their home. There was little in the way of furniture or personal items inside the structure. In a flash of lightning, the Rangers noticed a small bunker against the wall at the end of the bed.

Calog told Nhan to tell the couple that they would not be harmed, that he and his companions had only entered their home to get out of the rain. While Nhan carried on a conversation with the two frightened peasants, Calog set up security, posting Lastine in the doorway facing the distant wood-line and Crabb in the back door facing the berm.

Lastine obtained the Starlight scope that Martin had brought out on the mission. He was using it to keep his eyes on the distant lights still glowing in the tree-line 300 meters away. He continued observing the lights for an hour and a half while the storm raged unrelentingly outside the hut. Nhan had been periodically talking to the owners of the hut to reassure them that the soldiers would leave as soon as the storm ended.

Lastine stood and stepped forward into the open doorway to get a better look at the distant lights. There was a nearby flash of lightning just as he reached the opening. In that brief moment of illumination, he saw what he thought was Nhan standing just outside the door 2 meters to the right. He thought to himself: 'What in the hell is Nhan doing outside in the rain?'

The surprise of seeing Nhan outside the building forced Lastine to take a step back inside the hut. He had a .45 caliber pistol in a holster on his belt and a parachute flare taped to his right leg. In the confusion of the moment he forgot both and reached back for the M79 grenade-launcher he always carried on patrol, then realized that he had an HE (high-explosive) round in the chamber. Holding the weapon in front of him, he waited for the next bolt of lightning. It came immediately and revealed the poncho-clad form of an NVA soldier silhouetted in the open doorway. In that brief instant, both men froze. Then the enemy soldier turned and ran to the left at a 45-degree angle toward the corner of the distant tree-line.

The first thing that flashed through the ATL's mind was 'An HE round has to rotate five times before it's armed. This guy is too close.' He dropped the weapon and tore at the parachute flare taped to his lower leg. He quickly popped off the cap, shoved it onto the other end of the tube against the striker pin, then stepped over the threshold of the doorway to slam the flare against the ground. Unknown to Lastine, the floor of the hut was 4in higher than the ground just outside the door. When he stooped to launch the flare, instead of slamming it almost vertically into the ground to impact the striker, the misjudgment caused him to jam the flare down hard but on a 30-degree angle, launching it almost horizontally in the general direction of the fleeing NVA. The flare whooshed out of the tube, but never reached an altitude higher than 15ft above the ground. It finally plopped harmlessly into the muddy rice paddy long before the parachute had a chance to deploy.

Somewhat embarrassed, Lastine jumped back through the open doorway, grabbed his grenade-launcher from the hard-packed earthen floor, turned and fired the 40mm round in the general direction that the NVA had fled. As the round exploded 30 meters out in the paddy, another flash of lightning revealed several more poncho-clad NVA a few meters back from the right corner of the hut. Once again, Lastine turned and dove back inside the building. Bear in mind that no one inside the hut except Lastine knew what was happening. In the mad scramble that followed, several rounds from an enemy automatic weapon suddenly tore through the bamboo walls of the hut. Miraculously, no one inside was hit. The rest of the team, suddenly realizing the danger, rushed to cover the two open doorways.

In the darkness inside the hut the Rangers hugged the ground, weapons at the ready, waiting for the enemy assault that they knew had to come at any moment. There was no time to flee, and no place to go even if they could. The NVA were just outside the building. The team remained in place for several minutes and when nothing happened, Calog whispered to his Rangers to prepare to charge out to the paddy dike 100 meters to their front. It was the only place that might offer them cover from an enemy assault. Seconds later, the team burst through the front door, expecting to have to fight their way through massed NVA waiting in the darkness, only to discover that no one was there. The NVA, not knowing for certain what they were dealing with, had decided that safety was the better part of valor and had abandoned the field of battle.

The Rangers continued running through the muddy paddy until they reached the dike where they separated and spread out over its 100-meter span. Keeping the dike between them and the wood-line 200 meters away, they prepared to fend off an assault from the enemy troops behind the lights they had observed earlier. Calog guessed that the NVA they had just tangled with back at the hut had probably been a smaller contingent that had come from the tree-line to the hut for the same reason the Rangers had, to get out of the rain. They had been just as surprised to find the Rangers inside as the Rangers had been to find them outside. When they didn't follow up the initial contact and were gone when he and his teammates charged out of the hut, Calog figured they must have fled back to the tree-line and were probably at that very moment telling their comrades about the small group of American soldiers hiding in the hut on the other side of the rice paddy. Calog knew that they would be coming soon.

An hour passed, then they saw a string of eight to ten lights moving out of the woods on each flank. Lastine and Calog had taken up positions anchoring the opposite ends of the paddy dike that spanned the field facing the wood-line. This put both the team leader and the assistant team leader directly in front of the NVA columns now moving toward them. The Rangers watched silently as the lights file continued to move in their direction. Calog estimated that there was roughly 10 meters between each of the lights. If there was another man between each one without a light, it meant that he and his teammates were facing an NVA platoon and were outnumbered better than five to one. He could also see that the lights were not casting beams, which indicated they were lanterns and not flashlights. If this was indeed the case, the enemy soldiers would not be able to see the Rangers until they were right on top of their positions.

The two strings of lights continued to move slowly down along the sides of the field, each group keeping pace with their comrades on the opposite side, until they finally reached the paddy dike where the Rangers lay waiting. The enemy paused there for several minutes. Finally, from each side of the field, two single lights detached themselves from the others and began moving very slowly and cautiously down the dike toward the waiting Rangers. Calog and Lastine, on the opposite ends of the dike, would be the first to make contact. Realizing that the two leaders would be facing the enemy assaults alone, Martin slipped quietly in next to Lastine and whispered in his ear: 'If we don't make it out of here, it's been nice knowing you.'

Some 20 meters from Calog on the right side of the dike and the same distance from Lastine and Martin on the left side, the NVA soldiers behind the lights stopped. Nearly a full minute passed while the Rangers waited breathlessly, their weapons ready to fire. Suddenly, the enemy soldiers turned around and retraced their steps back down the dike to the sides of the field. There was another brief pause, then all the lights turned back toward the wood-line 200 meters away.

The pouring rain drowned out the audible collective sighs of relief from the team as the last of the lanterns finally disappeared into the trees. By some divine twist of Fate, the Rangers had managed to avoid a confrontation with an overpowering number of enemy troops during the dark, stormy night. Each of them realized that if there had been a battle, there would have been no extraction, no reinforcements, no air support, and no escape and evasion. It would have been a battle to the end, with the odds of survival stacked against them.

Calog stood and moved down the dike, gathering up his teammates as he went. Satisfied that he had left no one behind, he led them back across the center of the muddy paddy. When they reached the darkened hut, they went in the front door and right out the back door, not stopping until they reached the berm where they had first set up earlier in the evening. It was just after midnight and the rain and thunder had yet to let up.

The weather cleared just after dawn, revealing the promise of a bright and beautiful day ahead. Calog called the relay team and requested an immediate extraction, giving them the coordinates of an open field 200 meters away.

The six men climbed wearily aboard the Huey when it touched down thirty minutes later. It had been a long and sleepless night, filled with fear and apprehension. On the flight back to Dong Tam, Lastine thought about the Vietnamese couple whose peace and quiet they had so rudely interrupted. Their lives, like the lives of the Rangers and the enemy soldiers in the tree-line, had somehow become forever intertwined during that stormy night. None of them would ever be the same.

Chapter Forty-Six

For the next seven days I spent most of my time drinking beer in the club and shooting the bull with my fellow Rangers. The mess hall was too far to walk, so I made my meals in my room on Frosty's hotplate. My parents had sent a couple of care packages containing canned goods and Supply had generously provided me with a good selection of dehydrated LRRP rations.

I visited Lieutenant Bill Anderson in his hooch one day. He offered me a beer and we sat and talked about a lot of things. He had a VC flag hanging on the wall next to an AK-47 and a set of enemy web gear he had captured on a mission he had led. He was a great officer who didn't let his rank interfere with the way he felt about his soldiers. I had a lot of respect for him, and I liked to think he felt the same way about me.

I never made any of the mandatory company formations. No one ever said anything about my lack of participation. It was pretty much an accepted fact that I was to be left to my own schedule as my wound healed.

As the wound slowly began to improve, I attended some of the films that were shown on the outdoor screen in the company area. It was not so much that I found them enjoyable, but they did manage to take my mind off the boredom and help to pass the time away.

A couple of weeks after my return to the company, I heard someone screaming in the company outhouse. Curious, I went to investigate and saw that a crowd had already gathered. They found one of the Rangers standing up, straddling one of the toilet seats. Beneath him on the floor an irritated cobra lay coiled ready to strike. One of the soldier's teammates quickly dispatched the serpent with his M16. Seconds later, the terrified Ranger ran out of the outhouse with his hands over his ears. Everyone began laughing at the spectacle.

As the time passed, I began to realize that something was wrong with me. At first, I couldn't figure out what it was, but I finally admitted to myself that I was suffering from combat withdrawal. Over the past ten months I had been involved in a lot of action and, without realizing it, I had grown just flat out physically and mentally exhausted. I had reached the point that I just wasn't coping with it at all. In my mind, I knew I wanted to return to Tan An and rejoin my team, but my body knew that I wasn't ready yet. I had gone back to see my doctor as ordered, only to have him tell me that he wouldn't release me until I had made a full recovery. My mind was also affected. I could tell that my self-confidence and mental acuity had reached a low point.

Frosty, my roommate, had kept his promise to share his bottle of whisky with me, saying that the hard liquor would help me heal faster. I enjoyed the older warrior's company. His well-honed sense of humor kept me in stitches...no pun intended.

I began to take stock of my own mortality. Mike Calog and Dennis Lastine had just survived a very close call. I, too, had made it through a few of those during my tour. For the first time, I realized that survival in combat was not only a matter of ability and prowess, but also a generous supply of good old luck. Ability and prowess were things over which you had some control, but your supply of luck was in the hands of Fate, and Fate was a fickle partner. You never knew for certain how much luck you had been allotted or when that allotment would run out. You only knew that it was not infinite.

Chapter Forty-Seven

By 20 June I was beginning to feel my old self again. The wound was healing nicely, and I was a week away from returning to the med station to have my sutures removed. I had stopped taking the pain pills the doctor had given me. A week after my return to the Company my pain was tolerable and mixing pain medication and alcohol was always a bad idea. I had found myself spending more and more time with Frosty. He had seen a lot of action while serving in Vietnam during a previous tour and was a master at telling war stories. We had finished off his bottle of whisky during my first few days back in the unit, but somewhere, somehow, Frosty had managed to find a suitable replacement. That night, Frosty, Mike Calog and I met up at the Club and spent the evening drinking and discussing the war. I asked Frosty if he intended to make the Army a career. He laughed and told me that he was getting out at the end of his current enlistment. He had talked to some 'spooks' about becoming a mercenary. He said that there were several 'brush-fire' wars heating up in Africa and the pay was too good to pass up.

I crapped out sometime around 2230 hours, excused myself and headed for my bunk. It had been a long day and I was bushed. Frosty and Mike finally closed the bar down at 0200 hours.

Frosty was up two hours later at 0400 to gather his teammates for a first-light Parakeet flight out near the Cambodian border. Not long into the mission, their LOH pilot spotted several VC fleeing along a narrow tree-line and radioed his sighting to the Huey flying high overhead. As the LOH scout helicopter buzzed the enemy soldiers to keep them in sight, the slick banked around and dropped the team off in a clearing less than 60 meters behind them. Frosty was the first Ranger to exit the chopper and immediately began pursuing the VC. Some 50 meters from the LZ, he paused and looked back to see if his teammates were behind him. At that moment, one of the VC turned and fired a single, off-hand round from his battered M1 carbine. It had to be a lucky shot. The .30 caliber bullet hit Frosty in the back just above his right kidney, tore through the bottom lobe of both lungs and exited his right side. He was spewing frothy blood from his lips as his teammates moved in and surrounded him. While they tried their best to stop the bleeding, Staff Sergeant Herbert 'Frosty' Frost bled out in a grassy field near the Cambodian border.

I took the news of his death very hard. The one guy in Vietnam that I believed was 'bullet-proof' had been killed by a lucky shot from a fleeing skinny little Viet Cong guerrilla. It didn't seem possible that the tough old warrior, a survivor of many a battle, could have died in such a way.

I had told Frosty the night before he was killed that I was planning on staying in the Army and doing my twenty years before moving on to something else. I knew that if I extended for six months, there would be a good chance that I'd make E-7 (Sergeant First Class) before I returned to the States. Now that he was gone, I questioned if it was such a good idea after all.

I mulled it over for several days, then decided that it was the best thing I had going for me. I went to the orderly room, told the clerk to prepare the paperwork and extended for an additional six months in Vietnam. This earned me a two-week leave back to the States before I had to begin serving my extension. My leave was due to begin on the anniversary date of my arrival in Vietnam so I had a few days to kill before going back to the States. I can't say that I looked forward to leaving the unit, although I knew it would probably be good for me to return to a civilized society for a breather. I was still suffering from physical and emotional exhaustion and a break in the action might be just what I needed.

Chapter Forty-Eight

A few days before my departure, Team 1-4 got a warning order for an overnight recon mission into the 'Bowling Alley', a fertile 4-mile-long valley out near the Plain of Reeds. The valley was approximately 12 klicks north-west of Tan An. The only cover in the 'Bowling Alley' was the narrow tree-lines running along the 'gutters' or outer perimeters of the valley. The center was occupied by dozens of rice paddies, broken only by the earthen paddy dikes that walled them off from each other. A few thatched hooches dotted the area, providing shelter for the Vietnamese villagers who planted and maintained the verdant fields.

Few Ranger teams survived long without being compromised in the 'Bowling Alley'. The local Viet Cong maintained a sizeable force in the valley, protecting the peasant farmers and making sure that they got their share of the annual rice harvest. Typically, when a Ranger patrol attempted to insert into the 'Bowling Alley' they would take fire on arrival or shortly thereafter.

Team 1-4's TL, Sergeant Gary Winkler, was an experienced warrior. He had volunteered for the Rangers after spending the better part of his tour with an infantry company. His ATL, Sergeant Roger Rudder, was also a seasoned soldier who had just graduated from MACV Recondo School at Nha Trang. The two Rangers decided to make an overflight of the valley, hoping to find a landing zone far enough away from the bordering tree-lines to give them a chance to get on the ground and into some cover without being spotted. They alerted the rest of their team to the upcoming mission, then climbed aboard the Huey slick to check out their AO.

While the NCOs were out over the valley, Specialist Fourth Class Frank Canibano, Specialist Fourth Class Dan Stouffer, Specialist Fourth Class Rich Marz and Private First Class Jerry Voris dressed in their cammies, applied their 'war paint', grabbed their gear and waited.

An hour later, Winkler and Rudder returned and gathered their teammates for the mid-morning insertion. Their mission was to recon the center of the valley to determine if the VC were there in force awaiting the upcoming rice harvest.

The Huey approached the valley from the western end, flying nap of the earth to confuse watchers on the ground. Flaring to a brief hover a few feet above the water near the edge of a large rice paddy, the aircraft waited less than ten seconds while the six camouflaged Rangers dropped from the skids into the flooded field. They huddled in a loose circle while the helicopter lifted out and returned to base.

As the low drone of the departing Huey died out in the distance, it was replaced by the sharp 'CRACK-POW...CRACK-POW' of an enemy sniper firing from a tree-line 400 meters away. Almost immediately, a second sniper opened fire from another location in the same tree-line. The six Rangers moved rapidly out into the center of the rice paddy to put some distance between themselves and the enemy sharp-shooters. At maximum effective range for the Viet Cong weapons, the patrol stopped and began to return fire into the wooded area. Winkler dropped to one knee in the shallow water and called for a fire mission from a nearby artillery base. As the 105mm HE rounds began bursting among the trees, Winkler told Rudder to use the other radio and call for gunships to follow up the fire mission. Several artillery salvos failed to halt the enemy fire, so when the two gunships arrived on station, Winkler called a halt from the heavy guns and instructed the Cobras to 'light up' the wood-line.

It was growing late in the day when the gunships finally depleted their ordnance and returned to base. The Rangers were surprised when the enemy once again began to fire on the team after the helicopters had departed. Winkler ordered up another fire mission, intent on blasting the surviving VC into oblivion.

Thirty minutes later, the Ranger TL radioed his CO to discuss the situation, then made the decision to continue the mission. He opted to move the team to the reverse slope of a large berm directly across the rice paddy from the tree-line where they had taken fire and set up a defense perimeter for the night. There was a small thatched hut on the crest of the berm to use as a reference point as they moved out in the growing darkness. Every thirty meters, Winkler stopped the team to look through the Starlight scope to get his bearings on the hooch. When they finally reached it, Rudder spread the patrol out along the berm while Winkler called in a sitrep.

A half-hour passed quietly. Winkler was observing the distant tree-line when he suddenly saw twenty-five to thirty enemy soldiers step out of it and begin moving across the rice paddy on line. They were at least 300 meters away, but were heading directly for the patrol's position.

Realizing that the six Rangers were outnumbered five to one and that it would be impossible to place accurate fire on the assaulting VC in the dark of the night, Winkler ordered his men to open fire on the enemy before they closed the distance. On his signal, three of the team members opened up with their M16s, while Winkler and Voris began lobbing 40mm grenade rounds through their rifle-mounted M203s and Stouffer put down an even heavier barrage with his M79. The exploding grenades and the automatic fire from the M16s stopped the enemy assault line dead in its tracks, forcing the VC to take cover behind a couple of paddy dikes to their front. For the next two hours, the two elements exchanged fire, the Americans attempting to keep the VC from continuing their assault and the VC intent on doing just that.

Out of 40mm rounds and running low on 5.56 ammo, Winkler knew there was little chance the patrol could make it through the night. He would have to call for a night extraction. The team leader radioed for gunships to hold off the VC to permit a Huey slick to slip in and extract his team. It was just after midnight when the gunships arrived on station. The Rangers marked their position with a flashing strobe light. Winkler called the gunships and told them that he would fire a magazine of tracer rounds into the area where the VC had taken cover in order to mark their location. Rudder observed the enemy positions through the Starlight scope and coached Winkler on where to place the tracer rounds. Halfway through the magazine, Winkler's rounds began impacting along the paddy dike where the VC had taken cover.

On their first two passes the Cobras blazed away with their mini-guns directly into the impact area of the team leader's tracers, then came back around a third and fourth time, launching their deadly missiles into the same area. Unable to observe the effectiveness of the air strikes, Winkler ordered the gunships to keep it up while the team was being extracted.

Minutes later, the patrol heard the unmistakable sound of an approaching Huey slick vectoring in on their strobe light. Hovering 3ft over the rice paddy directly in front of the Rangers' position, the Huey held steady while the six warriors scrambled over the berm and climbed aboard. Winkler did a final head count to make sure no one had been left behind, then yelled to the pilot: 'We're good to go.'

Safely back at Tan An, Winkler thanked the aircrew for a job well done, then dismissed his teammates while he and Rudder headed for the Ops shed to give newly-promoted Captain Zapata their mission briefing. It was a good night for Team 1-4. Not many Ranger patrols could say they had lasted almost an entire day in the 'Bowling Alley'.

Chapter Forty-Nine

I spent most of my two-week leave with my family. It was good to be with my parents again. Although the time passed too quickly, it was long enough for me to know it was time for me to get back to the war. It's funny how you miss combat, but it's a fact. I don't know if it's the thrill of the danger, the anticipation of battle or the camaraderie with one's fellow warriors, but you indeed yearn for it when you're out of it.

I reported back to the Oakland Army Base to catch my flight back to Vietnam. I was sitting in the terminal waiting for the announcement of my departing flight when I heard my name being called over the loudspeaker. I was ordered to report to the main departure desk. I grabbed my carry-on bag and walked across the terminal to the counter where I announced myself to the SFC behind the counter. He looked at me and said: 'Sergeant Thayer, I have your orders to report to Fort Leonard Wood.'

I was shocked, and blurted out: 'There must be a mistake. I'm headed back to Vietnam.' The stocky NCO shook his head, looked down at my orders and replied: 'No mistake. You've been given a compassionate reassignment to Fort Leonard Wood. It says here that you need to call home right away. Your father is in the hospital. He had a heart attack.'

I was speechless. For the first time in my life, I felt real fear. My dad could be dying, and I had to get home. I snapped back to reality when the Admin NCO offered me the use of the telephone on his desk behind the counter. When I finally got in touch with my mom, she told me that my dad was okay. He had had a mild heart attack and was in the hospital, but he would be able to go home in a few days. Relieved, I told her that I was in California and had gotten orders assigning me to Fort Leonard Wood, close to their home. I said I would be on my way and should be there in a day. I thanked the sergeant for the use of his phone and said: 'Well, I guess Fort Leonard Wood is in Missouri!' He nodded and replied: 'It was the last time I checked. You need to report in there in one week.' He handed me my orders and plane tickets and wished me good luck.

When I arrived home the next morning, I went immediately to the hospital and spoke to the doctor about my dad's condition. He told me that my father had suffered a mild heart attack. He had put him on medication that should regulate his heart. When I asked what had brought it on, he told me that it was likely the stress of me returning to Vietnam and the fact that I had been wounded three times during my first tour, combined with grief over the loss of my older brother in the Second World War. It had been too much for his heart to deal with. He then admitted to me that he had been instrumental in obtaining my compassionate reassignment. My mother had found out that he was a friend of a very influential senator who was the friend of a very influential general, and in a matter of a few hours, new orders had been cut assigning me to Fort Leonard Wood, Missouri so that I could be close to my family. I was a little angry at first, then after thinking about it for a minute or two, I knew it was okay with me, knowing that my dad would be pleased that I would be safe and close to him.

I spent the next week at home with my family. When Dad was finally discharged and sent home, I made sure that we shared some valuable time together, something we had both overlooked during my teenage years. I was at peace for the first time in a long time. My war was behind me, and I had survived it. I had time to reflect on the events of the previous year: the 'close calls', the excitement, the wounds, the broken marriage, the loss of my daughter, the guilt of surviving, and the deaths of comrades. It was a burden that would haunt me the rest of my life. There would be no more war for me, but at the same time, I knew there would be no real peace either.

Chapter Fifty

A week later I reported to Fort Leonard Wood Headquarters Company. When I checked in, a young lieutenant greeted me and announced: 'Ah, Staff Sergeant Thayer, we've been expecting you. The general wants to see you.'

I followed him into the general's office, came to attention and saluted as he introduced me. The general returned my salute, got up from his desk, came around to the front and shook my hand. 'Good to meet you, Sergeant Thayer. I've been looking over your file. Very impressive. I would like you to work here in Headquarters if you are agreeable.' Somewhat overwhelmed, I answered: 'Yes, Sir. Thank you very much, Sir.' He told me that the lieutenant would get me squared away, nodded and dismissed the two of us with a wave of his hand.

The lieutenant took me back out to the admin office and showed me to a desk. He pointed to it and said:

> This is yours. Your duty will be to check in personnel transferring into the post. You will also be in charge of assigning body escorts from permanent party personnel, arrange their plane tickets, and brief them on where to go to meet their casualties. Their job description requires them to remain with the bodies at all times, from Stateside arrival to the grave site. They are to assist the families in any way they can. Commissioned officers and non-commissioned military personnel from the nearest Army posts will be assigned to handle the graveside services. In addition to these tasks, there may be other duties that pop up from time to time. Any questions, Sergeant?

I shook my head. 'No, Sir, not at this time. But can I reserve the right to rescind my decision at a later time? I'm sure something will pop up.' He smiled and answered: 'Sure. No problem.'

I finished processing in, then went to find a temporary bunk in Headquarters barracks. I spent the next three days taking care of personal business. I turned in a request to live off-post and it was quickly approved. Satisfied that I was squared away, I left post and went to an auto dealership where I had spotted a dark, metallic green Plymouth Roadrunner on my way in. I took it for a lengthy test drive and decided that I had to have it. With my purchase completed, I also bought a 750cc motorcycle to ride back and forth to the post when the weather permitted. Jimmy Thayer was now mobile. Funny thing about bikes…over the next several years I found that I was frequently trading them in for something bigger and more powerful.

Next, I had to obtain insurance on both vehicles, get decals enabling me to drive them on post, and get my Missouri driver's license. When that was accomplished, I leased a mobile home a few miles off-post that was exceptionally nice compared to the places I had called home over the past two years. There was another mobile home just behind mine. It was occupied by another soldier who was a mechanic in the post motor pool. He lived there with his wife and a couple of young children. I introduced myself and promised him that I would do my best to keep the noise down.

A few days later, I was sitting at my desk going over some paperwork when I heard the door open. There was a sign on my desk that read: 'INCOMING PERSONNEL REPORT HERE'. Not looking up from my paperwork, I heard someone walk up to my desk and come to a stop in front of it. Satisfied that I had made him wait the appropriate amount of time worthy of my rank, I finally looked up to see the familiar face of Sergeant Mike Calog with a shit-eating grin plastered across his face.

'What in the heck are you doing here?' I blurted out, surprised to see my fellow Ranger standing there. He answered: 'And what in the heck are you doing here?' I said: 'I got a compassionate reassignment. What's your excuse?' He shrugged his shoulders and retorted: 'Got me. I have no idea.' It was great to see him again. We had shared some unforgettable times in the 9th Division's Ranger Company.

Over the next year, Mike and I spent a lot of our off-days drinking in the local bars, chasing the local beauties and getting in a few non-verbal disagreements with the local folks and other soldiers. I don't know if we were testing our manhood or we were just short of patience, but somehow or other the two of us managed to avoid getting tossed into the local calaboose or the post stockade. It was great knowing that someone you could trust always 'had your six', and I'm sure that Mike felt the same way about me. Fifty years later we are still the best of friends.

Chapter Fifty-One

I spent the next two months working at Post Headquarters assigning body escorts and arranging their travel to and from. The lieutenant was right about additional duties; however, there was never enough work to keep me busy. I soon found myself getting very bored with the job. I was a warrior, not a pencil-pusher. The tedious paperwork, the total lack of excitement and the ennui began to take a toll on my motivation. I found myself hitting the local bars after work looking for a chance to vent and blow off a little pent-up steam. My buddy, Mike Calog, was in the same boat as me. A training post was a poor substitute for the thrill of a small unit patrolling in 'Indian country'. We both knew it would only be a matter of time before we would manage to get ourselves in some serious trouble.

I decided that for a change of pace I would take the next body escort myself that came to my desk. At least it would get me out of the office for a while. I met the casualty at the Oakland Army Terminal and escorted it to its destination. I spent a lot of time between the funeral parlor and the family making sure that everything went well. When the funeral was over, the family requested that I remain with them for the next two days.

A few days after I returned to Fort Leonard Wood and resumed my duties, the Post Commander called me into his office and told me that he had just received a letter of appreciation from the captain in charge of the military personnel who handled the service, lauding my performance. He read it aloud to me and when he finished, he said: 'Well done, Sergeant Thayer.'

A few days later, the feeling of confinement became almost overwhelming. I went to see the Post Commander again and told him that I thought I would be more effective if I were assigned to the Vietnam Training Unit on Post. I explained that I wasn't comfortable doing paperwork and felt that my experience in the field would benefit the trainees preparing to go to Vietnam. The general thought for a moment,

159

then said he understood where I was coming from. He admitted that he hated to lose me, but he agreed to approve my reassignment.

I left his office more relieved than I had hoped. I truly believed that the change of work and scenery would help get me through the final year of my enlistment. I was no longer sure about remaining in the Army. The ability to make E-7 in the next few months had been quashed by my compassionate reassignment. Only serving another six months to a year in Vietnam with the Rangers could make that a possibility. My fast track to promotion was gone. My dad's health issues also had a lot to do with any decision I had to make concerning a military career. I honestly felt that I should remain near my folks; to be there should things begin to go downhill for them. They were both reaching the age where they would soon need someone's help. As the youngest son, with no family to support, I felt it was up to me to provide that help.

Chapter Fifty-Two

I spent the rest of my time at Fort Leonard Wood working at the Vietnam Training Company. Our mission was to train young recruits about the dangers they would face when they arrived in-country and to help them deal with the coming stress of combat. One of my duties was to set up ambushes on motorized convoys. I would place explosive charges along a road where a three-truck convoy would soon be traveling. I would also position a group of local 'VC' along the hillside facing the road. When the convoy rolled into the 'kill zone', I would detonate the charges, while my enemy contingent would open fire on the trucks. The trucks would slam to a stop when the charges went off, permitting the troops to exit the vehicles and charge the enemy soldiers engaging them on the hillside flanking the road. It wasn't very realistic since the charges were weak and the rounds were blanks, but it was only meant to give the recruits a taste of what battle was like. In a real situation, most of them would likely be cowering behind the vehicles instead of charging the enemy.

One day, I made the mistake of putting a little too much explosive in the lead charge. When I blew it, it sent a rock through the radiator of the lead vehicle and lifted the front end off the ground a foot or two. My training officer, a young second lieutenant, clambered out of the truck holding his hands over his ears. The look he gave me was not one of admiration.

A few days later, we ambushed another convoy. When the recruits came charging out of the trucks and assaulted up the wooded hillside, I began pulling the strings on artillery simulators and tossing them among the attackers. There was little actual danger to the troops. The simulators were noisy but would not cause bodily injury unless you fell on one just before it exploded.

Suddenly, one young recruit dove to the ground when he heard a nearby simulator whistle in and land next to him. The lieutenant saw him go down next to the hissing device. The officer ran over, grabbed the recruit by the back of his shirt and the seat of his pants and tossed him away from the simulator. Unfortunately, it exploded before the young officer could retreat, blowing his helmet liner off and knocking his glasses askew. The lieutenant slowly stood erect, straightened his glasses, then looked up at me and said: 'Sergeant Thayer, I do believe you are trying to kill me.' I answered: 'No, Sir, it just looks that way.' I laughed, walked over and put my arm around his shoulders and added: 'Too many witnesses here, L-T.'

Thank God the lieutenant was a good-natured guy.

Chapter Fifty-Three

On 12 July, the one-year anniversary of the day I was last wounded in Vietnam, I began experiencing some discomfort in my chest in the area of my sternum. I decided to go on sick call and see the doctor to determine what was causing the problem. We discussed my previous wounds and he decided to order an X-ray to see if the shrapnel that had been left in my chest was the source of my discomfort. After looking at the X-ray, he couldn't say definitively if the metal was the cause of my pain, but he offered to remove it if I wanted it done. I told him that if there was any chance the shrapnel was the problem, I would like it taken out. He agreed and scheduled me for surgery.

A few days later, I reported to General Leonard Wood Army Hospital. The staff prepped me for surgery and the anesthetist arrived to put me to sleep. While I was out, the surgeon cut around my sternum and removed the offending piece of metal. I woke up a short time later to find myself lying on a gurney out in a hallway. It felt as if an elephant was squatting on my chest. The pain near my solar plexus was so severe I could hardly breathe. I tried to open my eyes and sit up on the gurney, but it was more of a struggle than I could handle at the time. Finally, I managed to sit up.

A medic came up to me in the hallway and said: 'The doctor said to contact someone from your unit and have them come to the hospital to pick you up.' If I had had the strength, I would have laughed in his face. As it was, I could only gasp weakly and mutter: 'Okay, get me to a phone.'

I made the call, and an orderly took over and got me back to my room. He helped me dress, then wheeled me out to the front of the hospital to await my ride. A short time later, a jeep arrived and took me back to the company orderly room. The captain came out of his office and said: 'Thayer, what in the world are you doing here?' I answered: 'Sir, the doctor released me and I didn't know what else to do.' 'Well I know what to do,' he growled and handed me a phone. 'Call your folks.'

I made the call and told my mom and dad to come and get me. My CO gave me two weeks of medical leave and ordered me to go home to heal before I had to report back for duty.

My parents drove me to their home, then took me to see their family doctor. He could not believe that the Army doctor had discharged me right after the surgery without even giving me a prescription for pain medication. He wrote one for me and told me to go home and rest for the next two weeks. My dad dropped my mom and I off at their home, then went to the local drug store to fill the prescription. I couldn't lay in a bed without pain, so I spent the next two weeks in my dad's recliner. At the end of that period, I had healed well enough that I was able to return to Fort Leonard Wood and resume my duties out on the combat range.

Chapter Fifty-Four

As my enlistment drew to a close, I began to receive a lot of pressure from everyone in my family to leave the service and return to civilian life. The war in Vietnam was winding down, but there was still time for me to pull another tour in-country. My brothers Don, Mel and Ray had served in the Second World War. Ray had been killed in action. Brothers Mel, Bob and John had served in Korea. Mel had been blown out of a jeep and his legs had been paralyzed. The Army had been unable to evacuate the wounded at the time, so he had been forced to remain hidden in a cave with other casualties for a few weeks until the military could medevac them to the rear. Fortunately for him, the feeling in his legs had returned by that time.

I had been wounded three times in a single year and my parents were afraid that if I re-enlisted, I would have to go back to Vietnam. I was the last of seven children. My mom and dad were in their mid-40s when I was born. Now they were in their 60s and they needed me close by.

Out of respect for my parents, I finally made the decision to leave the Army when my enlistment ran out in January 1971. I would seek a job in law enforcement. After submitting my application to several local police departments, I was offered a position with a department in south-west Missouri, close enough to my parents to be able to help them when they needed it. I applied and was accepted for a thirty-day early-out and began a new career in law enforcement, which would last until my retirement. My warrior days had come to an end, but like all of us who had answered our nation's call, I would never forget the experience. It was the finest time in my life. It was also the worst time in my life. I have never been as alive as I was during that amazing year when I was part of a band of true warriors. I would do it all over again.

Epilogue

The officers and enlisted men of E Company, 50th Infantry (LRP) and E Company, 75th Infantry (Ranger), 9th Infantry Division served valiantly during the five years the division fought in Vietnam. I am proud to say that I had the privilege of serving with some of the finest soldiers in the world during my year in the unit. I've always believed that in my day, the motto of the Ranger Regiment 'Rangers Lead the Way' was constantly reaffirmed, yet I qualify it by adding: 'but when they reached their objective, they found that the LRPs had already been there and gone.'

In the five years we operated in South-East Asia, our unit lost 26 young men killed in action out of the almost 500 who served in our ranks. No one knew them all, yet we all knew some of them. They were our friends, our comrades, our brothers. It is difficult to suffer the loss of comrades in battle. To those of us who survived the war, they will always be remembered as young warriors, never to be subject to the ravages of age and infirmity, and we survivors endure. We honor their memories every time we gather. As long as one of us remains alive, they will never be forgotten.

I trust that this book will answer many questions for friends and family that I have been unable or unwilling to explain over the years. Like all warriors, we have a difficult time sharing our experiences with the uninitiated. It is not pride or self-righteousness that prevents our sharing, but an inability to verbally describe the horrors we have seen and experienced. Forgive us for that inability. It is not something we have selectively chosen. Maybe in writing my words will provide insight and understanding. It has been a difficult experience gathering my thoughts and memories from fifty years of 'cold storage'; thoughts and memories that I have suppressed.

In 2015, the Long Range Reconnaissance Association was formed during a rally held in Branson, Missouri. Every year since our founding we have gathered in June at the same location to share the special brotherhood that exists among us. Long Range Recon Patrol (LRRP), Long Range Patrol (LRP), Vietnam Rangers and Long Range Surveillance (LRS) join together for four days of camaraderie. The organization is open to all of those who served in a long-range patrol-type unit from the Cold War, Vietnam, Bosnia, Iraq and Afghanistan.

Over the years I have often wondered what had happened to Jim Martens, the wounded point man that I had once carried from the battlefield. Every time I spotted someone with a cane or a missing leg, I thought of him. Then one day in 2017 I found him on Facebook. I got his phone number and called him. We planned on meeting at the LRRA Rally in Branson that year. When we finally met again that warm June day, it proved to be a truly memorable experience. He had recovered from his wound and had led a successful, happy life.

The rally is a wondrous event, with the old Nam vets mingling with the younger warriors who have so proudly carried on our legacy. The US Army has phased out the long-range surveillance units, believing that drones and satellites can accomplish the missions we had performed, but someday, maybe when the need for us arises once again, the Army will reconsider its decision and bring back the teams. Until then, we will continue to gather each year to keep the brotherhood alive.

I want to thank my fellow LRPs and Rangers who helped me put this book together, especially those who directly contributed. A special thanks to a good friend, brother and author, Gary Linderer for his help with the edit and his moral support in completing this work.

In Memoriam

NAME	DATE OF DEATH	UNIT
SGT Ray M. Gallardo	11/08/1967	E Co., 50th Inf. (LRP)
PFC Thomas W. Hodge	01/24/1968	E Co., 50th Inf. (LRP)
PFC George J. House	02/11/1968	E Co., 50th Inf. (LRP)
SSGT Kenneth R. Lancaster	03/06/1968	E Co., 50th Inf. (LRP)
SP4 William F. Piaskowski	03/14/1968	E Co., 50th Inf. (LRP)

(continued)

TANGO 1-1

NAME	DATE OF DEATH	UNIT
MSG Joseph M. Jones	04/16/1968	E Co., 50th Inf. (LRP)
SSGT Johnston Dunlop	04/16/1968	E Co., 50th Inf. (LRP)
SP4 Herbert L. Vaughn	05/25/1968	E Co., 50th Inf. (LRP)
PFC James L. Dillard III	09/13/1968	E Co., 50th Inf. (LRP)
SSGT Herbert P. Cho	09/25/1968	E Co., 50th Inf. (LRP)
CPL Robert J. Loehlein Jr	09/25/1968	E Co., 50th Inf. (LRP)
PFC Ronald K. Moore	11/04/1968	E Co., 50th Inf. (LRP)
SGT Joseph P. Castagna	12/21/1968	E Co., 50th Inf. (LRP)
SP4 Richard R. Bellwood	01/25/1969	E Co., 50th Inf. (LRP)
SGT Roman G. Mason	01/27/1969	E Co., 50th Inf. (LRP)
SP4 Leon D. Moore	01/27/1969	E Co., 50th Inf. (LRP)
1LT Richard V. Thompson	01/27/1969	E Co., 50th Inf. (LRP)
SP4 Irwin L. Edelman	02/18/1969	E Co., 75th Inf. (Ranger)
SP4 Warren G. Lizotte	02/26/1969	E Co., 75th Inf. (Ranger)
SGT Lonnie D. Evans Jr	04/10/1969	E Co., 75th Inf. (Ranger)
SP4 Michael C. Volheim	05/29/1969	E Co., 75th Inf. (Ranger)
SSGT Curtis R. Daniels	05/29/1969	E Co., 75th Inf. (Ranger)
SSGT Herbert C. Frost	06/21/1969	E Co., 75th Inf. (Ranger)
SP4 Jonathan L. Lamm	02/11/1970	E Co., 75th Inf. (Ranger)
SGT Robert L. Bryan	07/13/1970	E Co., 75th Inf. (Ranger)
1LT Mark J. Toschik	08/11/1970	E Co., 75th Inf. (Ranger)